DISCOVERING THE FOLKLORE AND TRADITIONS OF MARRIAGE

George Monger

SHIRE PUBLICATIONS

Published in Great Britain in 2011 by Shire Publications Ltd, Midland House,
West Way, Botley, Oxford OX2 0PH, United Kingdom.
44-02 23rd Street, Suite 219, Long Island City, NY 11101, USA.
E-mail: shire@shirebooks.co.uk   www.shirebooks.co.uk
© 2011 George Monger.

Every attempt has been made by the Publishers to secure the appropriate
permissions for materials reproduced in this book. If there has been any
oversight we will be happy to rectify the situation and a written submission
should be made to the Publishers.

A CIP catalogue record for this book is available from the British Library.

Shire Discovering no. 304.   ISBN-13: 978 0 74780 819 0

George Monger has asserted his right under the Copyright, Designs and Patents
Act, 1988, to be identified as the author of this book.

Designed by Tony Truscott Designs and typeset in Garamond
Printed in China through Worldprint Ltd.

11 12 13 14 15 10 9 8 7 6 5 4 3 2 1

COVER:

Signing the Register, by Edmund Blair-Leighton (1853–1922).
(Bristol City Museum and Art Gallery, UK / The Bridgeman Art Library)

ACKNOWLEDGEMENTS
Over the years I have been lucky to have met a good many people who have
freely shared their knowledge and experience of wedding customs and
traditions, too many to mention – therefore a blanket thank you to you all.
My thanks also go to Eileen Monger for photographing and preparing the
illustrations on pages 8, 17, 62, 77, 84, 86 and 91.

CONTENTS

INTRODUCTION

Despite an apparent drop in the number of weddings in Britain, marriage is still an aspiration of the majority of young people, and many brides put a great deal of effort and money into the wedding to make the 'big day' special. The concept of the wedding as the 'big day' is almost universal and it is considered one of life's 'rites of passage'. In rural Ireland, for example, an unmarried man or woman of any age was not considered a proper adult and would be treated almost as a child.

The wedding is bound about with a great deal of custom, superstition and convention, and these customs and ceremonies can be seen to have at least one of four functions: to fulfil a legal requirement; to enable a public recognition of the marriage; to help the couple set up home as an independent unit; and to wish the couple luck and good fortune.

The convention of the ceremony is established by law – ecclesiastical, communal practice and governmental legislation. The observance of some customs may confer regularity of the marriage in the communal mind; for example, there is an account of a choirboy who, despite being present throughout the marriage service, was convinced that the bride's father was the groom because the father had mistakenly paid off the boys who were barring the church gates, instead of the groom who, by custom, should have paid to let them through.

Customs and traditions have also arisen from the legal and statutory parts of the marriage process, as can be seen with traditional practices and superstitious beliefs that have arisen around the calling of the banns on three successive Sundays before the wedding. In Great Britain, unless a special licence is obtained, the celebration of a wedding should legally take place in public before witnesses (there are some cultures where marriage is undertaken surreptitiously), establishing the couple as a unit within the community. Legislation has had a profound influence on marriage practices and changing traditions, the most influential being Lord Hardwick's Marriage Act of 1754, which effectively stopped irregular marriages and opened up the marriage market at Gretna Green.

In times with a low literacy level the public performance of marriage rituals and customs embedded the event in the collective memory. Being a public event, the wedding and the marriage could be subject to malevolent influences and thoughts – always a danger at life-changing events. So there are a number of superstitions and practices intended to bring good luck to the couple and to avert bad luck.

There are, too, practices designed to help the couple establish their new partnership and set up home, obviously to help ensure that the couple are not a drain on the community. Examples include practices where members of the community donate a piece of furniture or household goods to the couple, the Welsh bidding customs and the 'penny wedding'. These practices continue today with the giving of wedding presents, the bridal shower in the United States and the Greek practice of pinning money on the bride and groom at the reception. Of course, commercial interests have become involved, for example department stores holding wedding present lists (and providing recommendations for items to be on the list), and the production of the wedding cake. It is interesting that in recent times some couples have asked for money instead of the 'traditional' wedding present. This has caused some debate in wedding magazines, newspapers, radio and television with a certain amount of adverse comment about this development. However, this is not a new idea – the 'penny wedding', for example, was one where the guests would donate money to the couple to help pay for the wedding and to help them set up home. Over the last 150 years the wedding industry has developed, building on fashion, and there are etiquette books that prescribe how the preparations and the celebrations should be carried out. Wedding magazines too give advice and ideas on how to make the wedding particularly memorable, and wedding fairs are held somewhere most weeks, where providers of 'necessary' services ply their wares.

The customs and traditions of marriage cover a wide range of practices. Some traditional practices and beliefs are localised; some, which appear to be local and peculiarly British, share similarities with customs and traditions in other cultures. Some apparently old traditions and practices (such as the white 'fairy tale' wedding dress) are more rooted in fashion than tradition – not all customs and traditions have origins that are lost in the mists of time. We can in some of the marriage customs see a form of continuity and change – the ideas behind the practice remain but the performance alters. True traditions are not set in stone.

This book describes customs and superstitions surrounding the whole area of love and marriage (and divorce) in Great Britain. It is not uncommon today for brides to borrow traditions from other cultures, such as the giving of sugared almonds to the guests, borrowed from Greek tradition, and decorating the hands with henna, from Muslim and Hindu traditions. A general overview is given, but there will be some elements of marriage and weddings which may have been missed in this book. It is a form of introduction; the further reading section at the end should enable the reader to fill the gaps.

OF LOVE AND COURTSHIP

Divinations

'Whom shall I marry?' is probably a question asked as often as, 'Will I get married?' To answer the first question a girl (usually) may try one of a number of divinations to find the occupation or even see an image of her future husband. Divinations were often performed at significant times and often at midnight, and there were a number of regional and local variations. A simple divination carried out at Hallowe'en is to peel an apple so that the peel is removed in one strip. The peel is then thrown over the left shoulder; this should land in the shape of her future husband's initial. Here two magical elements converge: Hallowe'en was a time when the barriers between the living and the dead and between our world and the world of the supernatural fell; and the apple, which had mystical significance.

On Hallowe'en night it is said that if a girl sits looking into the mirror, lit by a single candle and eating an apple, she will see the apparition of her future husband in the mirror. Alternatively, she could sit at her mirror, brushing her hair at midnight, with the room again lit only by a single candle; the reflected image of her future husband will appear in the mirror.

Hallowe'en was also called 'nutcrack night' because chestnuts were roasted on the fire, giving rise to another Hallowe'en divination. If a girl had two or more suitors she would put the chestnuts to roast in a line and name each with the name of the suitors and the middle one with her name. If a nut cracked and jumped away from her then the suitor with that name would not be true; the one that stayed and was burnt alongside the chestnut with her name would remain true and they would consequently marry.

'Whom will I marry?' Nutcrack night divination. Drawing from Chambers' *The Book of Days*, 1863.

This same divination was also performed on St Mark's Eve (24 April).

In Scotland, girls would pray to St Andrew on St Andrew's Day to get a husband. St Agnes' Eve (20 January) was a well-known time for divinations and celebrated in John Keats' poem *The Eve of St Agnes*:

> They told how upon St Agnes' Eve,
> Young virgins might have visions of delight,
> And soft adorings from their love receive
> Upon the honey'd middle of the night,
> If ceremonies due they did aright;

The ceremonies mentioned by Keats involved the girl (usually) going supperless to bed, backwards and without speaking or looking from side to side. She would see a vision of her future husband during the night. For the more hardy and determined an alternative was to hard boil an egg, remove the egg, fill the shell with salt then eat the shell and salt, without taking a drink, and go to bed backwards reciting the rhyme:

> Sweet St Agnes, work thy fast,
> If ever I be to marry man
> Or even man to marry me,
> I hope this night to see.

She would then dream of her future husband.

An alternative divination from Tyneside, north-east England, again for St Agnes' Eve but for a man, was to eat a raw herring whole so that he would dream of his future wife.

But midnight is a good magical time and the scarier the situation for a divination the better. Sowing hempseed in the churchyard at midnight, for example, chanting the rhyme: 'Hempseed I sow, hempseed grow / He that is to marry me / Come after me and mow' would result in the apparition of a girl's future husband coming behind making the motions of a reaper cutting the hemp.

A divination from Northern Ireland required the girl to pick nine pieces of yarrow; on going to bed that night she should throw seven of the leaves out of the window reciting the rhyme:

> Good morrow sweet yarrow, good morrow to thee,
> I hope before morning my true love to see.
> The colour of his hair, and the clothes he will wear,
> And the words he will say when he comes to court me.

The last two pieces of yarrow were then placed under her pillow and she would dream of her future husband.

A variation on this, again from Northern Ireland, was for a girl to pick nine leaves of yarrow on May Eve, reciting a similar verse to the one above and putting the leaves under her pillow.

Placing a piece of wedding cake under the pillow at night is said to result in a girl dreaming of her future husband. Sometimes an additional ritual is required and the cake should be passed three times through a wedding ring.

Another bedtime ritual was for a girl to place her shoes in the shape of a 'T' beside her bed, and say goodnight seven times out loud before getting into bed backwards with her eyes shut. She would then dream of her future husband. A correspondent to the *Daily Mirror* newspaper in 1971 explained that she carried out this ritual and that night dreamt of the film star Douglas Fairbanks Jnr. Ten years later she married a man who her friends said was his double.

St Valentine's day, now known as a day for lovers (see below) was, as would be expected, also a time for divinations. If bay leaves were pinned to the four corners and the centre of the pillow a girl would dream of her future husband. A girl could write the names of potential husbands on slips of paper, roll them into clay balls and drop them into water. The first name that rose up out of the clay would be her Valentine. Or, if the first person a girl met when out of the house was a man, she would be married in three months, whereas if she met a woman, she would not be married that year.

St Valentine's day

St Valentine's day, 14 February, is now well known as the day for lovers and for expressing, often anonymously, amorous feelings for another person.

Although traditionally 14 February was the time when the birds mate, it is not clear whether this belief is a product of the St Valentine's day traditions or whether the amorous associations arise from this belief.

There is little to connect St Valentine with a day for lovers apart from the time of his martyrdom. St Valentine was a priest in Rome who was executed in the third century, by being beaten with clubs and then beheaded, for refusing to renounce his Christian faith during the persecutions during the time of Claudius II. However, it is also said that he was martyred for allowing Christian soldiers to marry in spite of the ban imposed by Claudius II.

Whatever the truth, his execution apparently took place during the Roman festival of *Lupercalia* – a festival of youth – during which boys would draw lots with the names of girls for them to accompany during the festival of Februata-Juno on 15 February.

The tradition of drawing lots in this manner was familiar well into eighteenth-century England. The traveller Francis Misson in his *Memoirs and Observations on His Travels over England* (1698) recorded a custom where an equal number of young men and young women would gather and each would write their name on a piece of paper. Misson wrote:

> On the Eve of St Valentine's Day the young folks in England and Scotland, by a very ancient custom, celebrate a little festival. An equal number of maids and bachelors get together; each writes their true or some feigned name upon separate billets, which they roll up, and draw by way of lots, the maids taking the men's billets and the men the maids'; so that each of the young men lights upon a girl that he calls his *valentine*, and each of the girls upon a young man whom she calls hers. By this means each has two valentines; but the man sticks faster to the valentine that has fallen to him than to the valentine to whom he has fallen. Fortune having thus divided the company into so many couples, the valentines give balls and treats to their mistresses, wear their billets several days upon their bosoms or sleeves, and this little sport often ends in love.

But this custom was not confined to the unmarried. In his diary for 14 February 1667 Samuel Pepys wrote:

> This morning came up to my wife's bedside (I being up dressing myself) little Will Mercer to be her valentine, and brought her name written upon blue paper in gold letters, done by himself, very pretty; and we were both well pleased with it. But I am also this year my wife's valentine and it will cost me £5; but that I must have laid out if we had not been valentines.

A few days later he noted that he had been drawn as a valentine by 'Mrs Pierces's little girl' – which presumably required a much cheaper gift obligation as he continued, 'which I was not sorry for, it easing me of something more that I must have given to others'.

Remarking on the jewels of a Miss Stuart, Pepys noted:

> The Duke of York, being once her valentine, did give her a jewel of about £800; and my Lord Mandeville, her valentine this year, a ring of about £300.

Such generous gifts would of course not be normal amongst the wider population, but this gift-giving custom was obviously widespread and was a tradition maintained in Norfolk well into the twentieth century. On St Valentine's eve it was the custom for packages to be deposited on the doorstep of the recipient labelled only with 'St Valentine's love' or 'Good morrow, Valentine'. Along with serious gifts there were also sham packages which start out as large parcels that grow smaller as the wrapping layers are removed to reveal a motto such as 'Happy is he who expects nothing, and he will not be disappointed.'

Over time the present-giving became a gift from 'Jack Valentine' or 'Mr. Valentine' to children on Valentine's eve. Trick packages, known as 'snatch Valentines', were also placed on doorsteps; these were attached to string so that the parcel could be whisked away when the door was opened.

There was also a tradition for children to go to the big houses and businesses singing a Valentine's day song and they were rewarded with gifts or coins thrown from the windows. Parson James Woodforde, rector of Weston Longville, Norfolk, from 1773 noted in his diary that he gave a penny to all the children in his parish under the age of fourteen.

Children's Valentine's day customs were not, however, confined to Norfolk. In places in Suffolk children were given the day off school, a penny and a bun for singing a Valentine's day song:

> Good morning, Valentine / Comb your hair, / As I do mine. / Two before / And two behind / Good morning, Valentine. / The roses red / The violets blue / The pinks are sweet / And so are you / If you'll be mine / I'll be thine / Good morning, Valentine.

Similar customs took place in Northumberland where children went from house to house 'valentining' (singing a Valentine's song):

> Good morrow, Valentine!
> Please give me a Valentine
> I'll be yours, if ye'll be mine,
> Good morrow, Valentine!

A Worcestershire custom was for boys to go from house to house singing a valentine's couplet and being rewarded with apples which were later cut and fried in fritters.

In Rutland children and old folk were given lozenge-shaped buns, known as *shittles* on this day and in Northamptonshire

Hand-made Valentines from Narberth, Pembrokeshire. (National Museum of Wales)

godparents gave sweet currant buns, called 'Valentine's buns', to their godchildren on the Sundays before and after St Valentine's day.

However, these customs have all but died out and the day is now dedicated to lovers. The first written Valentine's message was believed to have been sent in 1684, but the sending of messages of love on this day did not begin to gain any popularity until the mid-eighteenth century and may have contributed to the decline in the practice of giving Valentine's day gifts.

Until around the 1840s hand-made Valentine's day cards would be sent; however, in this first half of the nineteenth century mass-produced cards became available. In 1855 around 800,000 cards were sent through the post and in 1882 over 1.5 million were sent. There was, however, a drop in card numbers during the 1860s along with a view that St Valentine's day observance had lost its way. Robert Chambers in his *Book of Days* (1863) wrote:

> Valentine's Day is now almost everywhere a much degenerated festival, the only observance of note consisting merely of the sending of jocular anonymous letters to parties whom one wishes to *quiz*, and this confined to the humbler classes. The approach of the day is now heralded by the appearance in the print-sellers' shop windows of vast numbers of missives calculated for use on this occasion, each generally consisting of a single sheet of post paper, on the first page of which is seen some ridiculous coloured caricature of the male or female figure, with a few burlesque verses below. More rarely, the print is of a sentimental kind, such as a view of Hymen's altar, with a pair undergoing initiation into wedded happiness before it, while Cupid flutters above, and hearts transfixed with his darts decorate the corners. Maid-servants and young fellows interchange such epistles with each other on the 14th February, no doubt conceiving that the joke is amazingly good; ... Such is nearly the whole extent of the observances now peculiar to St Valentines Day.

In 1913 Elizabeth Mary Wright in her book *Rustic Speech and Folklore* wrote, 'The custom of writing and of sending Valentines is out of fashion and there remains little to mark the day.'

Clearly the observance of St Valentine's day by sending a message of love, sometimes anonymously (and sometimes as a 'joke'), has survived and is now an even bigger and more commercial event than in past times – to such an extent that anti-Valentine's cards and presents have been produced as a protest against the commercialisation of the festival.

Courtship

In societies with a free choice of love and marriage partner, meeting, getting to know and courting members of the opposite sex is essential.

In times past there may have been fewer opportunities for young men and women to meet and get to know each other. In many walks of life men and women were quite separated in work and in leisure. For example, until the latter half of the twentieth century few women frequented public houses – it was viewed generally as a male social space and those women who did go to a public house would be unlikely to go to the bar, or be allowed to buy a drink.

There were social events and communal activities which would allow for meetings and attachments – such as harvest time in rural communities, markets and fairs, dances and holidays. But within the context of these events a 'matchmaker' or go-between could be involved. In Ireland this was especially so and in many areas there would be a recognised matchmaker who could be called upon by anybody in the community.

'Lonely Hearts' advertising columns in newspapers and magazines, and dating and matrimonial agencies could also be resorted to. Such agencies are not a modern phenomenon. In 1797 there appeared a newspaper advertisement for 'A New and Original Grand Matrimonial Intercourse Institution' and in 1839 an advertisement for a marriage broker proclaimed:

> Portfolio for the inspection of ladies, and which will contain certain copies of the letters, without name or address, from

> gentlemen of rank and fortune, gentlemen of private fortune,
> officers in the army and navy, and other professional gentlemen
> of high respectability and fortune, who are sincerely desirous of
> uniting themselves in marriage with ladies of respectability.

The end of the twentieth century and the beginning of the twenty-first century saw Internet matrimonial agencies for most cultures, including the Muslim community where marriages have traditionally been arranged by the parents.

In some towns, notably industrial towns, there were areas where the young people would congregate on a Saturday or Sunday to 'eye up' and meet each other. In East Lancashire, Friday night was definitely not a night for courting – if a couple did meet on a Friday the friends and neighbours of the couple would create a hullabaloo and give them a hard time. A children's rhyme from Cornwall designates Saturday as the courting night:

> Saturday night is courting night,
> I wish the time was come
> For my house is swept and sanded,
> So all my work is done.

Between around 1890 and 1939 Saturday and Sunday nights in Oldham Street, Manchester, became the 'Monkey-Rank' where single young men and women would promenade hoping to meet and 'click' with someone. Similarly in Chorley, Lancashire, 'the Drag' was the venue for this promenade – but there was a certain segregation in force with the 'tuppence-ha'penny side' (2½d) for factory workers and the 'tanner side' ('tanner' being the slang term for 6d) for the office girls and clerks. This was not unusual and similar events and demarcations were found in other towns and cities.

In many respects social changes caused by the two world wars broke down some of the barriers which prevented young people meeting. The development of coffee bars and youth clubs also helped break these barriers. Moreover, it became more and more possible for a couple to get some privacy to get to know each other.

Historical novels and writers such as Jane Austen give the impression that courtship could be very controlled and bound about with various manners and customs and required the permission of the woman's parents (notably the father). There were indeed certain rituals and indications of intentions to go a-courting.

A Sussex tradition was for a man who intended to go courting to carry a 'honeysuckle stick' (a hazel stick that has been disfigured by honeysuckle growing up the tree, leaving deep grooves and ridges in the bark) which signalled his intentions and was thought to bring him luck. The clinging honeysuckle was thought to be symbolic of a woman's love and faithfulness.

A seventeenth-century account of a courtship in the East Riding of Yorkshire demonstrated a highly formalised approach. A man, or his father, wrote to the girl's father to enquire whether he would be welcome to visit the house. If the reply was favourable the man would visit twice to see whether the girl liked him. If she did on a third visit he would take a gift, a sort of token of the courtship – a piece of gold or a ring up to the value of about ten shillings. The next visit he would give her a pair of gloves. The courtship, if it was to result in marriage, would last about six months and such gift-giving suggests this courtship would be between a couple from fairly affluent families.

However, during the courtship of the less well-off tokens of affection were given to the woman by the man, such as carved wooden love spoons in Wales, carved knitting sheaths in the Yorkshire Dales and, in lace-making areas, carved or decorated lace bobbins.

A problem for a courting couple was often being able to meet and get to know each other with any privacy. However, there was a tradition of 'bundling',

A Welsh love spoon, given as a love token. (Author's collection)

or courting in bed, where the couple were allowed to spend the night together but with strict limitations. The couple would both wear their underwear or the woman would wear a shift that was secured to prevent any untoward activity. Securing a board or placing a bolster down the centre of the bed and even tying the girls' ankles together were also steps which were taken to maintain the couple's innocence.

Even with precautions it was not unusual for the first child to be born a few months after the wedding. However, in some communities, such as that of the Cornish miners where the whole family worked the 'family pit', pregnancy before marriage was an advantage: it proved fertility, thus ensuring the future of the family to work the pit.

Matchmaking and arranged marriages

Arranged marriage, an agreement between the parents of a couple for them to marry, is often associated with Muslim and Hindu practice. However, it is not unknown amongst the British gentry especially during the Middle Ages and well into the seventeenth century (and may even persist to the present day amongst some families); there are cases of children being espoused at a young age to be married when they are considered old enough (see Betrothal, page 19), to consolidate family or political alliances. Such arrangements between families had little input from the couple involved. The practice of arranged marriages is central to the widespread traditional ballad 'The Trees They Do Grow High':

> O father, dearest father, you've done me much wrong.
> You've tied me to a boy when you know he is too young.
> O daughter, dearest daughter, if you'll wait a little while
> A lady you shall be, while he's growing.
>
> And at the age of sixteen he was a married man
> And at the age of seventeen the father of a son,
> And at the age of eighteen the grass grew over him,
> And death had put an end to his growing.

It is worth noting that in many Muslim communities although a marriage may be arranged by the couple's parents, the couple do have some veto over the chosen partner.

If you had no family connections to arrange a marriage there was sometimes the local matchmaker who could bring people together, and there were marriage markets such as that still held at Lisdoonvarna in Co. Clare.

Betrothal or engagement

After a suitable courtship period it was usual for the man of the couple to ask permission of the woman's father for her 'hand in marriage'. So marriage would be a matter of agreement with the woman's parents. In recent years, when people often delay marriage, this little formality is often foregone. However, an unmarried man or woman was, until relatively recently, considered under the control of their father so could not get married without parental permission. In parts of Ireland the unmarried of any age would be treated as children, with few adults' rights.

The engagement is 'traditionally' sealed with a ring, usually a diamond ring. It is true that in 1477 Archduke Maximilian of Austria sealed his betrothal to Mary of Burgundy with a ring set with diamonds; this was far from the norm. The establishment of the diamond ring as *the* engagement ring is in fact a victory for diamond company De Beers. An advertising campaign in late 1930s America promoted the diamond engagement ring, suggesting that the diamond ring was a symbol of the love of the man for the woman and the corollary that the bigger the stone the greater his love. The campaign also established the rule of thumb that the engagement ring should cost two months' salary.

The giving of a ring has long been a symbol of everlasting love (the ring is symbolic in this respect because it has no beginning or end). The poet Robert Herrick (1591–1674) wrote, in his poem 'A Ring Presented to Julia':

Julia, I bring / To thee this ring, / Made for thy finger fit; /
To show by this / That our love is, / Or should be, like to it.

And in 1730 the poet George Woodward in his 'To Phoebe, presenting her with a ring', wrote:

> Accept, fair maid, this earnest of my love,
> Be this the type, let this my passion prove;
> Thus may our joy in endless circles run,
> Fresh as the light, and restless as the sun;
> Thus may our lives be one perpetual round,
> Nor care nor sorrow ever shall be found.

However, the giving of a ring specifically to mark an engagement to marry appears to be a nineteenth-century phenomenon: John Cordy Jeaffreson in his *Brides and Bridals* (1872) wrote of 'the espousal ring, forerunner of our modern "engagement ring"'.

The engagement is a promise to marry and the engagement period a time for planning the wedding and collecting the basic items for establishing a household – although many young women would have been collecting such items for her 'bottom drawer' for a number of years already. If the modern engagement is a promise to marry, which can be relatively easily undone if the couple decide that they are incompatible, the older betrothal and espousal was much more binding.

We get the term 'spouse' for a marriage partner from the term 'espouse', which came to mean 'to wed' but at one time had the meaning of 'to make a contract to marry' – either immediately or sometime in the future – and was associated with formal ceremonies as solemn as the wedding itself. There were two forms of espousal, which hinged on the form of words used in the agreement. If the couple said 'I do take thee for my…' then the espousal was considered to be *de praesenti*, a binding contract that neither side could easily dissolve. There were, however, conditions which could allow, or even compel, the couple to break the contract. They were effectively married but without the status and rights of a married couple. If the couple said 'I will take thee for my …' then the espousal was considered to be *de futuro* – a promise to be married so that the couple were effectively in a marital no-man's land; they were neither married nor single. However, the couple could break the contract by mutual consent. If the couple consummated the relationship then they would not be able to break the contract because this would establish the contract in the present and they would therefore be considered married.

Espousal *de futuro* probably had more use when children of the landed families were promised to each other by their fathers to cement alliances and fortunes.

Presents were often exchanged between the couple at, and during, the espousal period; if the contract was broken the couple would have to return all presents given to each other, unless the contract was sealed with a kiss, in which case the woman would have to return only half the presents. One common present was a ring, which the woman would wear on her right hand. The wearing of the engagement ring on the right hand continued into the nineteenth century.

The gifts and tokens of affection given included gloves, shoes, coins and handkerchiefs. In the Yorkshire Dales it was common for carved and engraved knitting sheaths to be given and in lace-making areas engraved and decorated lace bobbins could be given.

However, whether or not such gifts or tokens were indicative of love, affection and indeed a marriage token rather than a gift in friendship depended very much on the context of the gift. The gift giving needed not be equal and the woman was not usually expected to initiate the gift giving, but this was a tactic sometimes used to trick a person into marrying. There are sixteenth-century ecclesiastical court accounts of women who gave tokens that were not reciprocated, and then maintained that a marriage contract had been entered into; similarly, there were cases of women being tricked into giving men small personal items only to find that they were claimed to be gifts and marriage tokens.

PREPARING FOR THE DAY

Choosing the time

Having made the decision to get married, when is the best time for the wedding? A marriage is a new beginning and as such a good time should be chosen to ensure good luck. The Church prohibited the solemnisation of marriage during the periods of Advent, Lent and Whitsuntide. Prohibited and permitted marriage periods were sometimes written at the beginning of the parish register, such as that of the church of Everton, Nottinghamshire:

> Advent marriage doth deny
> But Hilary gives thee liberty;
> Septuagesima says thee nay,
> Eight days from Easter says you may.
> Rogation bids thee to contain,
> But Trinity sets thee free again.

That Lent was a prohibited time for marriage is not a surprise. In Wales, for example, it was considered unlucky to be married at this time and there was a widespread saying:

> Marry in Lent / You'll live to repent.

In rural Ireland Shrove Tuesday, the last day before the restrictions of Lent, was a customary time for weddings.

Another couplet said:

> Who marries between sickle and scythe / Will never thrive.

The period of the year bracketed between the sickle and the scythe more or less corresponded with the church prohibitions – the sickle was used for the corn harvest and the scythe for the hay harvest. There was a belief in Ireland that a couple who married during the harvest period would spend all their lives gathering.

There may also be a feeling that the bright summer months were the best time for a marriage rather than the gloomy winter period, expressed in the couplet:

> Married in June
> Life will be one honeymoon.

It is sometimes said that the belief that June is the best time for a marriage goes back to ancient Roman times when Juno, wife of Jupiter, was especially honoured. As patroness of the young and goddess of marriage she would naturally look favourably on couples who married at this time and make them prosperous and especially happy.

On the other hand many books of wedding customs state that couples avoided the month of May because it was said to bring bad luck, often repeating the saying:

> Marry in May, and you'll rue the day.

Again the ancient Romans are blamed for this belief because this was the month that offerings were made to the dead and when mourning clothes were worn. The Roman writer Plutarch noted that Romans did not marry during the month of May.

However, analysis of yearly wedding statistics over several hundred years suggests that couples did not avoid May as a wedding month and indeed there was often a slight peak of weddings in May and September, which corresponded with seasonal payments when more people would have the money to be able to get married.

There are, too, a number of rhymes expressing the attributes of the days of the week:

> Monday for wealth (or health),
> Tuesday for health (or wealth),
> Wednesday the best day of all,
> Thursday for losses,
> Friday for crosses,
> And Saturday no luck at all.

A variation on this rhyme:

> Wed on Monday, always poor,
> Wed on Tuesday, wed once more,
> Wed on Wednesday, happy match,
> Wed on Thursday, splendid catch,
> Wed on Friday, poorly mated,
> Wed on Saturday, better waited.

It is unclear where these rhymes originated and how closely they were followed. In Orkney and Shetland, for example, Thursdays and Fridays were the most favoured days for a wedding. However, in the Lowlands of Scotland a Friday was not considered a propitious day but in Ross-shire a Friday was considered a good day for a wedding. It is interesting to note that the worst day of all – Saturday – has for most of the last hundred or so years been the most common day for a wedding.

Whichever day is chosen, since 1754 and Lord Hardwick's Marriage Act the wedding should take place in daylight before noon, until 1934 when this restriction was relaxed.

Wedding rings

A ring on the finger has long signified the married status of the wearer; indeed in the old ballad 'Little Musgrave and Lady Barnard' one verse runs:

> 'Ae nicht wi to sleep' he says,
> 'that wad breed meikle strife;
> For the ring on your white finger
> Shows you are Lord Barnard's wife'

Today the wedding ring is usually a band of gold but this was not always necessarily so. Most people could not afford a gold ring so sometimes any ring would do, but this did lead to sham and clandestine marriages using, for example, rings of rush. But it was not unknown for couples to hire a wedding ring.

The wedding ring is worn on the fourth digit of the left hand by tradition. The reason usually given is that it was believed that a vein or nerve ran from this finger straight to the heart. A sixteenth-century writer, Laevinus Lemnius, claimed to have revived women who had fainted by rubbing saffron onto the ring and pinching the wedding ring finger. This, he claimed, restored forces to the heart.

Another reason suggested for this finger is that the left hand is not used as much as the right hand and the ring finger can not be extended on its own so the ring is less likely to be damaged.

However, before the Reformation it seems that the wedding ring was generally worn on the right hand. Peter Heylyn in his *History of the Reformation* (1661) wrote:

> … that the man should put the wedding ring on the fourth
> finger on the left hand of the woman, and not on the right as
> hath been many hundreds of years continued.

However, eighteenth-century portraits of married women do not always show a wedding ring on the left hand and in the late sixteenth century and the seventeenth century it was fashionable to wear the wedding ring on the thumb.

During the Commonwealth Period (1649–60) when a Puritan Parliament ruled the country the use of the wedding ring was forbidden because of its 'heathenish origins'. Samuel Butler in his poem *Hudibras* (1663), which attacked the Puritan rule, wrote:

> Others were for abolishing
> That tool of matrimony, a Ring
> With which the unsanctified Bridegroom
> Is married only to a thumb.

Despite the ban on the ring (and on the use of the *Book of Common Prayer*) the Presbyterian minister of Finchingfield, Essex, performed the wedding of one of his daughters with the *Book of Common Prayer* and with a ring to ensure that she had a legal marriage and would not be returned to him.

There is a common belief that the giving and receiving of a ring ensured the legality of the marriage, although the retention of the ring was not considered absolutely necessary; it was not unknown for the church key, for example, to be used in lieu of a ring. In south-west Ireland there was a belief that it was necessary for a gold wedding ring to be used for the marriage to be legal.

A Yorkshire tradition was that it was lucky to be married with a borrowed ring. Some believe that the wedding ring should not be tried on before the wedding as this would tempt fate, although there are those who believe it could be tried on but not worn before the wedding.

It was unlucky to drop the ring before or during the ceremony and could foretell the early death of one of the couple. If the bride or groom drops the ring during the ceremony and it rolls away from the altar steps then that is a bad sign. If it comes to rest on a grave, the early death of one of the couple is predicted: if the grave is that of a woman then the bride will be the first to die; if the grave is that of a man then the groom will die first.

Most of these traditions usually refer to the ring given by the groom to the bride. During the twentieth century it became normal practice for the couple to exchange rings – it is not clear if these various ring beliefs are applicable to the groom's wedding ring, nor indeed if it has the healing powers of the bride's ring, which could be used to cure sore eyes, or a sty in the eye, by rubbing the affected eye with a wedding ring.

The wedding ring is said to signify the never-ending affection of the couple and gold symbolises the enduring nature of the marriage. Breakage or loss of the ring, therefore, would foretell the break-up of the marriage either through the death of the husband or the loss of his affections. The wearing away of the ring is also said to indicate that the marriage too is wearing away, but it is also said that as the wedding ring wears so the cares will wear away too.

Some believe that it is unlucky to remove the wedding ring after it has been placed on the finger in church although some believe that it is safe to remove the ring, if necessary, after the birth of the first child. If the ring should accidentally fall off, the bad luck can be avoided if the woman's husband replaces the ring on his wife's finger.

The wedding dress

The white silk, lace and tulle wedding dress that many brides wear has become almost symbolic of a wedding; however, such extravagant dresses did not become commonplace until the mid-twentieth century and is more a product of the wedding industry than of any traditions in this or any other country.

The myth of the white wedding has a long history. John Cordy Jeaffreson in his *Brides and Bridals* (1872) writes:

> From ancient of days our maidenly brides have arrayed themselves in robes of lustrous whiteness for the marriage ceremony.

In Oliver Goldsmith's play *The Good Natured Man* (1768) the maid says to the heroine:

> I wish you could take the white and silver to be married in, it's the worst luck in the world in anything but white.

However, most of the eighteenth- and nineteenth-century wedding dresses surviving in museums today are in colours other than white. Indeed the wedding clothes would often be the couple's best clothes, so it was sometimes difficult to identify the bride and groom amongst the guests. The bride would indicate her status with ribbons and favours attached to her dress. Sir George Head, in *A Home Tour through the Manufacturing Districts and Other Parts of England, Scotland and Ireland* (1840), describes a multiple wedding in the poorer parts of Manchester:

> ... as to the bride and grooms, as few were dressed in special costume, and all were very generally attended by friends and relatives, it was not easy to say which was which.

White as a symbol of purity and virginity, and the fashion for white dresses with their associated symbolism, developed during the eighteenth century, but this dress colour was available to, or practical for, relatively few people. The colour of the wedding dress has acquired symbolic significance according to the 'traditional' rhyme:

> Married in white, you have chosen all right;
> Married in grey, you will go far away;
> Married in black, you will wish yourself back;
> Married in red, you'd better be dead;
> Married in green, ashamed to be seen;
> Married in blue, you'll always be true;
> Married in pearl, you'll live in a whirl;
> Married in yellow, ashamed of the fellow;
> Married in brown, you'll live out of town;
> Married in pink, your spirits will sink.

Green is often said to be an unlucky colour because of its association with fairies – they did not like mortals wearing their colour – and some interpreted it as the colour of promiscuity; however, the colour green is also said to typify youth, hope and happiness.

Indeed, Mary Woodman's wedding etiquette book published in 1949 gave 'more correct' interpretations of colours which, according to the writer, 'for several centuries ... have been accepted as faithful portents – more or less – of the future'. In this book white is a symbol of purity and high virtues; green, of youth, hope and happiness; red a sign of vigour, passion and courage and violet suggests dignity, pride and high ideals.

In some places, such as Yorkshire and the Isle of Wight, blue was considered unlucky. This may have been because of the association of the Virgin Mary and the colour blue, which Catholics might consider only she should wear, and which Protestants might not like because of their opposition to Catholic reverence for the Virgin. In any event the bride should wear 'something old, something new, something borrowed, something blue'.

Although the distinctive wedding dress is more a product of the wedding industry, which developed during the nineteenth century, than of long tradition there are a number of superstitions that have become associated with the dress. The bride should not make her own dress, nor should she try on the complete outfit before the wedding day. There is also the well-known belief that it is unlucky for the groom to see his bride in the wedding dress before the wedding day.

At the other end of the dress scale it was not unknown for a woman to be married wearing only her shift or chemise, because it was believed that if the woman came to the wedding altar with nothing (partly or entirely divested of clothing) then her new husband would not be liable for any debts she may bring with her. On marriage the husband acquired an interest in her estate and consequently her debts too. An account from the 1547 parish register of Much Wenlock, Shropshire, notes:

> Here was wedded Thomas M. Smith and Alice Nycols, which wedded to him in her smock and bareheaded.

From Saddleworth, Derbyshire, there is a 1774 account of a bridegroom, a widower aged around thirty, marrying a widow of nearly seventy, who had some debts and he insisted that she wear only her shift. As the wedding took place in February, she became very cold and began to shiver uncontrollably so that the minister took pity on her and wrapped her in his coat.

For the groom there is little in the way of costume tradition and it has, in the past, changed with fashion. Like the bride he would wear his best clothes, which in the twentieth century was usually a suit. However, over the years and with increasing affluence it became customary for the groom, his best man and ushers to hire top hats and grey or black morning suits for the wedding, the type of outfit worn by the aristocracy and the well off in the past, and which became fashionable towards the end of the nineteenth century (although there was discussion concerning whether the coat should be a frock coat or tails). A description of the outfits worn by a bridegroom and his best man from *The Tailor and Cutter* in 1899 resembles the contemporary male costume promoted by specialist wedding outfitters:

> Black frock coat faced with silk. Double-breasted waistcoat of light colour and a dark tie, or a dark waistcoat with a light tie. Grey stripped cashmere trousers. Patent leather button boots. Pale tan kid gloves or of grey suede. Silk Hat.

However, it is interesting to note that earlier in the century the bridegroom's outfit would have been more flamboyant. A description from the *Ipswich Journal* for 1812 noted that the bridegroom wore a plain blue coat with yellow buttons, a white waistcoat, buff breeches and white stockings – the white waistcoat and stockings being characteristic of the wedding outfit. In his *Sketches by Boz*, Charles Dickens (1835) describes a bridegroom as wearing a blue coat with white trousers and Berlin gloves.

The veil

The veil is often considered an essential part of the bridal outfit and is sometimes said to have derived from the bridal canopy or 'care cloth' which was held over the couple during the Christian Anglo-Saxon wedding. However, the veil did not become part of the bridal outfit until the eighteenth century and did not become common until the nineteenth century. Writing in his diary on 7 February 1854 the Reverend Benjamin Armstrong, the vicar of East Dereham, Norfolk, noted that there was excitement in the parish because a certain Miss Dingle wore a veil at her wedding and that it was said to be the first seen in the parish.

The size and type of veil has been a matter of fashion. In the nineteenth century veils were very long and hung down behind the bride from her bonnet or head dress. It was not until the latter part of the nineteenth century that it became usual for the bride to enter the church with the veil covering her face. The practice of entering the church with the face covered and leaving with the face uncovered was a later refinement.

Veils were usually made from Brussels or Honiton lace and there was a tradition amongst the Nottingham lace embroiderers to take a long fair hair from one of the girls and work it into the veil. If the hair went through without breaking then a long and happy marriage for the couple was foretold. If the hair broke at the beginning of the process then the bride would be the first of the couple to die; if it broke at the end, then the husband would be the first to die.

It is considered bad luck to show the veil to anyone outside the bride's immediate family before the wedding and, except for fittings, should not be put on before the wedding morning. Even during the fitting it should not be worn with the wedding dress. If, for any reason, the bride should wear the veil before the wedding day she should not look in a mirror or else the marriage will be unhappy or the bridegroom will either desert her or else die before the wedding day. In some places it was believed that wearing her grandmother's veil would ensure that the bride would always have wealth.

On her wedding day the veil should be put on the bride's head by a happily married woman when she is ready to go to the church, and it is only then that she may look at herself in a mirror. If the veil is accidentally torn during the day, especially at the altar, then the bride would have good luck.

The wedding cake

The contemporary wedding cake is mainly a product of the nineteenth-century confectioner's art but is part of a continuing tradition. It is often said that the wedding cake as we know it developed after the Restoration of the English monarchy in 1660 when Charles II brought chefs from France who encased the traditional bridal cake, in the form of buns, in a shell of hardened white sugar decorated with toys and figures. This white crust could be easily broken to release the buns. However, such a confection was probably not widespread.

Spiced buns, made with sugar, eggs, milk and spices, were used in Elizabethan times and most likely before, and these were referred to as 'Bride-Cakes'. The poet Robert Herrick (1591–1674) wrote:

> This day, my Julia, thou must make,
> For mistress bride, the wedding cake:
> Knead but the dow, and it will be
> To paste of almonds turn'd by thee;
> Or kisse it thou, but once or twice,
> And for the bride-cake ther'l be spice.

This suggests that the bride-cake was a spiced cake covered with almond paste, and according to the poet Thomas Campion (1575–1620) in his poem 'Jack and Joan', which includes the line 'And trim with plums a bridal cake', it either contained or was trimmed with plums.

The diarist John Aubrey (1626–97) remembers as a child seeing a bride and groom kissing over a mound of bride-cakes towards the end of the wedding dinner. Earlier some of the buns may have been thrown over the heads of the bride and groom as they left the church. This appears to be a continuation of a tradition from the medieval period when thin grain biscuits were broken over the heads of the bride and groom. This is usually linked to a practice from ancient Rome where, it is said, the priest divided a wheaten cake between the bride and groom. This appears to give a link between the wheaten cake broken over the couple's heads and the scattering of grain over the couple as they leave the church.

Although there is little similarity between the bride-cake and the contemporary wedding cake there is a continuation of traditions extending into the twentieth century: it was still customary, especially in the northern counties, to throw a piece of the wedding cake, on a plate, over the bridal car after the wedding.

In the East Riding of Yorkshire as the bride and groom left the house for the church the groom was given a piece of wedding cake on a plate which he threw over the bride's head. The more pieces the plate broke into on landing the greater the luck the couple would have in their life. It was inauspicious if the plate did not break; if this happened a quick-witted bystander would stamp on the plate to preserve the couple's luck.

A practice in Goole, Yorkshire, was for the bride and groom to cut the wedding cake before the wedding; the rest of the cake was cut into pieces by a person deputed to stay at the house. On their return a plate of cake was thrown over the newly married couple. Again, the plate should break to bring the couple good luck.

If there were icing flowers on the cake, these would be given to a single girl to ensure that she would be married. In other parts of the country if a single girl kept a piece of the wedding cake, passed it through a wedding ring three or nine times and put it under her pillow at night she would dream of her future husband. In Shetland the bride-cake was sometimes known as 'Dreaming Bread' because of this tradition.

The custom of breaking the cake, or sometimes bread, was quite widespread in the north of England and Scotland. In the Scottish Borders it was a practice to throw shortbread over the couple when they entered their new home and in some places the bride's mother-in-law would break a cake or loaf of bread over the head of the newly married woman as she entered her new home. This was said to establish a good relationship between the two women. Similarly, a tradition from Ireland was for the bride's mother to break a cake over the woman's head to bring her luck and fertility.

The multi-tiered royal iced wedding cake came into vogue during the nineteenth century and as late as 1888 there seems to have been a distinction between the 'Bride-Cake' and the 'Wedding Cake' (there was a class for 'Wedding Cakes' and another for 'two-guinea bride-cakes' at the Universal Cookery and Food Exhibition in London in 1888).

Mrs Beeton in her *Book of Household Management* (1880) gave a recipe for a 'Bride' or 'Christening Cake' and the cheaper *Every-day Cookery and Housekeeping* recipe is simply for a 'Wedding Cake'. However, it is evident that Mrs Beeton considered that the name of the cake was dependent on the occasion for which it was made.

When multi-tiered wedding cakes first began to be developed at the end of the nineteenth century they were laid one upon the other. Decorative pillars were later produced so that the tiers could be separated and two, three and four tiers became the norm. However, this has led to extravagant many-tiered cakes being made. The *Romford Recorder* newspaper of 24 August 1973 reported a couple having a 27-tier cake (which was around 3 metres high). Apparently it was a 'tradition' in the bridegroom's family (the cake nearly collapsed twice before the couple arrived at the reception).

The bride and groom cutting the cake in public – a great photo-opportunity for the guests – is considered an important part of the reception. This is a fairly recent tradition: in some areas well into the twentieth century the cake was cut before the bride and groom went to church for the wedding; this ritual has developed its own traditions and folklore.

The bride should not be involved in the making of her wedding cake – this may have been promulgated by bakers and confectioners to ensure clients for their cakes. The bride should cut the first slice of the cake or else the marriage will be childless. When the bride and groom cut the cake together – the usual practice now – the partner whose hand is uppermost on the knife handle will be the dominant one in the partnership.

To ensure that her husband remains faithful to her throughout the marriage the bride should keep a portion of the cake. However, a tradition from North Yorkshire was for the bride to eat a piece of the wedding cake and then throw the rest of the slice over her shoulder to signify that the couple would always have enough and some to spare.

Finally, the top tier of the wedding cake was often kept to be the christening cake for the first child – a practice which is reminiscent of Mrs Beeton's book where there is no difference between the recipe for the wedding cake and the christening cake.

The banns

It is a legal requirement that the banns for marriage be published either in church on three successive Sundays or for a suitable period at the Registry Office local to each of the partners, so that any valid objections or impediments to the marriage can be made known. This requirement was embedded in Lord Hardwick's Marriage Act of 1754 where it became an offence to be married anywhere other than in a church or public chapel without the prior calling of the banns or without a special licence. This was an attempt to prevent elopements, clandestine marriages (Fleet weddings) and marriages to an unsuitable person or a 'gold digger'. Lord Hardwick's Act did not apply in Scotland, which led to the rise of Gretna Green as a marriage destination.

However, before Lord Hardwick's Act, Archbishop John Peckham had decreed in 1200 that the banns of marriage be published in church three times before the marriage. In 1215 the fourth Lateran Council ordered that the banns be published as part of canonical law. If the couple lived in different parishes then the banns should be read in both parishes and the wedding should not take place without a certificate of the reading of the banns from the curate of the church that was not being used for the ceremony.

Before 1754 if a priest officiated at a wedding without calling the banns on three successive Sundays he would be offending against ecclesiastical law and the church authorities could take action against the priest, but could not nullify the marriage. However, some clergy seem to have been prepared to bend ecclesiastical law. From the parish records of St Mary's Church, North Stifford, Essex, there is an entry for 28 October 1658:

> … were married Grace Heath and Thomas Ffish, strangers both, by Mr John Stone, Ministr of Greyse [Grays, in Essex], ye banns not published.

And in 1709 there were two entries which suggest rule bending:

> July 25 Edward Horniblew and Rose Holman banns thrice published and married the same day.

> October 16 William Roberts and Elizabeth Nelson banns 3 published and married the same day.

In the English folksong 'Come Write Me Down' from the singing of the Copper Family of Rottingdean, Sussex, the penultimate verse begins:

> To Church they went the very next day
> And were married by Asking as I've heard say…

To be 'asked' in church was one of several local terms for the calling of the banns; this is a term used in the *Book of Common Prayer*:

> And if the persons that are to be married dwell in divers Parishes, the Banns must be asked in both Parishes.'

It would therefore appear that the couple in the song were married according to the law and not by special licence or irregular means (for example, elopement).

Other local terms for having the banns read in church include being 'cried' in church; 'calling home'; being 'thrown over the rannal-bawk' (an iron beam in a kitchen chimney from which kettles were hung) and 'spurring'. In the north of England, a bell known as the 'spurring bell' was rung after the third reading of the banns to bring a blessing to the couple. The congregation would often shout 'God speed 'em well', but this was frowned upon by some members of the clergy and a vicar in one Yorkshire parish suppressed this customary expression of good will because it 'excited unseasonable mirth among the younger portion of the congregation'.

At one time if the couple called the wedding off after the third reading of the banns they could be fined by the clergy, as this was interpreted as a scorning of the Church. The reading of the banns was seen as the first stage of the marriage, similar to espousal, and if there were no objections to the union, that constituted an implied communal agreement to the marriage. Therefore, calling off the marriage at this stage may also be seen as a slight to the community and the couple could be further ostracised by the locals who might punish them by making 'rough music' (see page 92) against them.

As with many areas of wedding folklore superstitions have arisen associated with the reading of the banns. A Lincolnshire superstition was that if the bell tolled for the death of a married woman on the same day as the third reading of the banns then the bride would not live for one year of her married life.

A Perthshire belief was that it was unlucky for a couple to have their banns read during the end of one quarter of the year and to be married at the beginning of the next quarter. In a number of places it was considered unlucky for the engaged couple to hear their banns read. If they did so their first child would be born with learning difficulties or else all their children would be born deaf and dumb. In the Leeds area of Yorkshire the latter fate would be likely if the woman attended church when her banns were being read. As it is usual for the couple to be present when their banns are read in church it would appear that few have experienced any dire consequences.

Pre-marriage

In the days before the big day it is now customary for the friends and colleagues of the couple to mark their change from single to married status with some form of celebration.

Until relatively recently, it was assumed that if a woman had employment before getting married she would leave work after the wedding to become a full-time housewife. Indeed in some professions, such as teaching, the civil service, nursing, working at the BBC (from 1932) and many industries, there was, until the 1960s, a 'Marriage Bar' – a ban on the employment of married women. This is now unlawful under sex discrimination legislation.

However, this meant that the day a woman left work before her wedding would be her last day in employment. In a number of offices and factories this led to an event where the woman would be decorated with ribbons, streamers and paper rosettes; she could be paraded around the workplace, perhaps given gifts, and often, as she left work for the last time, be showered with confetti. She would of course be escorted or paraded home to make sure that she presented a spectacle for the other workers. In the Sheffield meat markets the woman would be paraded on a market barrow and could even be tied to a lamppost.

Ribbon girl, a bride-to-be being escorted home from work after the workplace celebrations in Romford, Essex, 1972.

Nowadays, if the woman works in an office her desk and computer may be decorated and if she uses a car or bicycle to get to work these too may be decorated by her workmates.

In Scotland the custom is more elaborate and known as 'Creeling the Bride' or 'Bosseller'. The coat belonging to the bride-to-be is decorated completely with paper flowers and a matching hat made. The bride-to-be is paraded through the streets; a chamber pot containing a piece of coal, silver and salt (coal representing warmth, silver wealth, and salt as never wanting for the necessities of life) is similarly decorated and at intervals during the parade she has to jump three times over the chamber

Bosseller, a Scottish pre-marriage celebration and ritual when the bride-to-be leaves work before her wedding. Kilmarnock, 1977. (William S. Paton)

pot, followed by her bridesmaids and the guests in the procession, who each jump once. A once common present given to the bridal couple in north-east Scotland was a chamber pot filled with salt and in the 1930s miniature chamber pots with a gilt inscription 'for me and my girl' and an eye on the bottom were for sale in Aberdeen market; these were often kept on the mantelshelf over the fireplace in the bedroom as a symbol of the marriage.

In factories in some of the Scottish Border towns, such as Hawick, the tradition was to blacken the feet of the prospective

Blacking of the bridegroom-to-be as part of the pre-wedding ritual. Fettercairn, Aberdeenshire, 2007. (Collections Picture Library)

bridegroom. Although the industrial pre-wedding customs are mainly women's customs there are a number of examples of a pre-wedding ceremony for men carried out at their workplace.

These events involved parading the man around the workplace, 'decorating' his jacket, and a great deal of after-work drinking. These events are reminiscent of the apprentice passing out customs when a young man (usually) finished his apprenticeship and could then begin the next phase of his working life.

There is an account of a similar custom from a London printing works recounted in a book by Charles Manby Smith (*The Working Man's Way in the World*, 1857) where a newly married man was paraded through the workplace accompanied by two workmates dressed as mock bride and bridegroom whilst everyone banged the workbenches to make a form of 'rough music'.

These customs mark the transition of the bride-to-be or the bridegroom from the single to the married state. The stag night, which developed to extreme levels during the twentieth century also marks a man's transition from the single to the married state, often characterised as losing his freedom – going from a carefree man with no ties to having responsibilities to supporting a wife and, in time, a family. So this is an alcohol-fuelled celebration with his male friends, now often organised by the Best Man, during which practical jokes are played, sometimes with an underlying level of malice (being tied naked to a lamppost and left, for example).

Arising from this tradition, the bride now has a hen night, an all-female affair, with dressing up, decorating the bride-to-be with L-plates and bunny ears, much alcohol and behaviour as bad as the men's on the stag night. In many respects the woman's celebration marks a greater change in freedom than the man's. His is a perceived loss of freedom; in practice the woman has traditionally lost more freedom on marriage. The hen night is not a totally new tradition: in Finland the bride-to-be has a *Polterabend* party, which involves

raucous parading through the streets with her friends on the night before the wedding.

These customs mark the event of the wedding within the work community and to a wider community and, when it was usual for the woman to leave work at marriage, to celebrate her last day at work. However, there are

A groom-to-be tied to a lamp-post as a pre-wedding prank, Belfast. (Collections Picture Library)

other pre-wedding events which were designed to help the couple in setting up their home. The wedding presents given by the guests are obviously intended to help set up the home and in America, Trinidad, New Zealand and Canada it is customary to have a 'bridal shower' – a party where the guests bring presents to help the couple furnish their home. This is usually a female affair; however, the Canadian version is particularly interesting.

The shower is organised by a friend or family member and is open to anyone in the community to attend. The event is advertised in the local newspaper and both men and women are invited. A collection is made for presentations during the evening and there are other collections for the couple during the evening and the proceeds from the sale of drinks also go to the couple.

This is reminiscent of the custom of 'bidding', which was found specifically in Wales and parts of Cumberland. Bidding entailed a couple of social events, one for the bride and one for the groom, which took place on the eve of the wedding and on the day itself where gifts and money were brought for the couple to help them set up home. An important feature of the bidding was that every donation was noted because the receiving couple were obliged to give a gift or donation of equal value at the bidding of the donor. A bidding debt could be passed on to relatives or friends and there are even examples of the debt being passed on in a will.

The community were invited to the bidding by a 'bidder' who would travel the area delivering either a written or a light-hearted verbal invitation. Food and drink would also be sold at the event to boost the funds for the couple. An advertisement for a bidding in 1803 in the *Cumberland Pacquet* suggests that there were other fund-raising events too:

> For whose amusement there will be various RACES, for prizes of different kinds; and among others a saddle, and Bridle: and a silver-tipt Hunting Horn for hounds to run for – There will also be leaping, Wrestling, etc. etc. … Commodious ROOMS are likewise engaged for DANCING PARTIES, in the Evening.

THE WEDDING DAY

'The Wedding' from *Old England*, 1860. (Collections Picture Library)

THE WEDDING DAY itself is associated with traditions and superstitions both old and not so old, and by legislation, the most notable being Lord Hardwick's Marriage Act of 1754. This Act, passed in 1753, was designed to prevent irregular and clandestine marriages, especially marriages of young heiresses and young men for their fortunes (as often happened especially in the Fleet area of London – a notorious place to go for a quick wedding, no questions asked).

The Act was highly contentious at the time because it gave the Church of England a great deal of control over marriage and made it more difficult for people to avoid the heavy taxes on marriage imposed by William III in a 1695 Act (it also taxed bachelors and childless widows over the age of twenty-five) to help fund the fighting of the French Wars. This had the effect of increasing the market for irregular marriages.

Hardwick's Act made it compulsory for a marriage to be officiated by a member of the Church of England clergy only after the publication of the banns, or by special licence, and only in the church or chapel where the banns had been published. Otherwise the marriage would be null and void and any clergy performing a marriage in contravention of the law would be transported to the Americas ('to some of His Majesty's plantation in America') for a period of fourteen years.

The Act did not apply in Scotland and there was an exception for Jews and Quakers; this was quite insulting for Protestant nonconformists and Catholics, who made strong representations against the Act but were unable to change the import of the law. During the passage of the bill many amendments were tabled to destroy it, including an exemption for Scotland. This exemption Lord Hardwick agreed to, to make sure his bill passed into law; this led to the development of the marriage business at Gretna Green, just over the English/Scottish border and therefore handy for runaway marriages.

Fleet weddings

Fleet weddings were notorious in seventeenth- and eighteenth-century England. The Fleet area of London, or Fleet Ditch, was the location of the notorious Fleet Prison, which held mainly debtors and those jailed for contempt of court.

In 1686 the Reverend Elliot was suspended for three years by the ecclesiastical authorities from his church, St James's, Duke's Place, London, for conducting weddings without calling the banns on three successive Sundays or with a special licence. By doing so he broke ecclesiastical law rather than civil law. He served about fifteen

Line drawing entitled 'Fleet Marriages' – an irregular wedding in London.
(Collections Picture Library)

months of his suspension during which time he continued to
conduct weddings at the Fleet Chapel. After he was returned to his
church marriages continued to be solemnised at the Fleet Chapel
over the next fifteen years by the Reverend Jeronimus Alley until he
was suspended by the Bishop of London. But these suspensions drew
attention to the fact that although ecclesiastical law prescribed that
marriage should take place in a parish church between certain hours
of the day and with the banns being proclaimed, a marriage
performed at night in a secular building and even without the
benefit of clergy was as valid in civil law.

This knowledge, along with the marriage taxes, led to many
couples going to the Fleet parsons, who would marry couples in their
own homes or in one of the many taverns in the Fleet area which had
established marriage rooms and touted for business. Not all marrying
houses were in inns or taverns – one, at least, was a barber's shop.

Between 1700 and 1754 there were no fewer than seventy Fleet
clergy and possibly up to one hundred. However, the Fleet area was
not the only place where irregular marriages took place, as noted
below.

Gretna Green

Gretna Green is the first town in Scotland over the English border and was therefore the immediate destination for eloping couples. By tradition couples were married 'over the anvil' by a 'blacksmith priest'; in practice most marriages during the heyday of Gretna took place in an inn or marriage house which would have handy bedrooms for the necessary consummation of the marriage (if the marriage was not consummated then it could be stopped or annulled) and the officiant was neither blacksmith nor priest. In Scotland the couple only had to declare themselves man and wife before two witnesses.

However, the self-styled 'priests' made a ceremony of the event. Robert Elliot, who claimed to have married 7,744 people between 1811 and 1839, gave the form of service he used in his memoirs, *The Gretna Green Memoirs*:

The Old Blacksmith's Shop and Marriage Room, Gretna Green. (Collections Picture Library)

The parties are first asked their names and places of abode; they are then asked to stand up, and inquired if they are both single persons: if the answer be in the affirmative the ceremony proceeds. Each is next asked, 'Did you come here of your own free will and accord?' Upon receiving an affirmative answer the 'priest' commences filling in the printed form of the certificate. The man is then asked 'Do you take this woman to be your lawful wedded wife, forsaking all other, keep to her as long as you both shall live?' He answers, 'I will'. Then the woman is asked the same question, which being answered the same, the woman then produces the ring which she gives to the man, who hands it to the 'priest'; the 'priest' then returns it to the man and orders him to put it on the fourth finger of the woman's left hand, repeating these words, 'With this ring I thee wed, with my body I thee worship, with all my worldly good I thee endow, in the name of the Father, Son and Holy Ghost, Amen.' They then take hold of each other's right hand, and the woman says, 'What God joins together let no man put asunder.' Then the 'priest' says, 'Forasmuch as this man and this woman have consented to go together by giving and

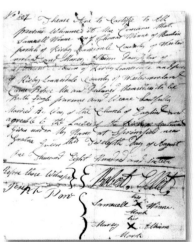

receiving a ring, I therefore declare them to be man and wife before God and these witnesses, in the name of the Father, Son and Holy Ghost. Amen.'

Elliot claimed that this form of service had been used by his predecessors

Gretna Green marriage certificate), 1816. (Ilfracombe Museum)

as 'priest'. He also mentioned the printed certificate of marriage. An example in Ilfracombe Museum, dating from 1816, was handwritten and the wording is very similar to that used by one of the early 'priests', John Pasley:

> This is to sartfay all persons that may be concerned at *A.B* from the parish of *C.* in the County of *D.* and *E.F.* from the parish of *G.* and in the county of *H.* and both comes before me and declaryed themselves both to be single persons and now mayried by the forme of the Kirk of Scotland and agreible to the Church of England, and ginie ondre my hand this 18th day of March 1793.

It is unclear when the tradition of being married over the anvil in the blacksmith's shop developed but it is interesting to note that the expression 'a blacksmith wedding' or 'blacksmith marriage' for a marriage of doubtful authenticity was known in the fifteenth century and may have originated from mainland Europe. In celebration of regular weddings blacksmiths were known to 'fire the anvil' where a small charge of gunpowder was put in the hole in the anvil and fired with a red-hot iron as a salute to the bridal party. This was a very dangerous custom and there is an account of the blacksmith at Bradfield, Essex, in the 1850s who was trying to force a plug of gunpowder into the hole using a sledgehammer. The resulting explosion blew the handle through his body, killing him instantly. However, the custom continued well into the twentieth century and there is an account of the anvil being fired at Greatham, County Durham, in 1936.

The blacksmith tradition at Gretna Green probably did not develop until around 1907 when a blacksmith's shop was converted into a shop for marriages and the sale of souvenirs and curios.

In 1927 the Laird of Gretna Green employed a man called Dick Rennison to work as the 'priest' in Gretna but his work was stopped in 1940 when Gretna Green marriages were declared illegal. It is still possible for romantically inclined couples to get married over the anvil at Gretna Green, but this is just a ceremony for show; the proper marriage now has to be performed by the town Registrar.

Gretna Green was not the only town over the Scottish border where couples went for a quick wedding. On the eastern side of the country Lamberton Tollbar, Berwickshire, was also a destination where until the middle of the nineteenth century there were at least eight or nine 'Toll priests' prepared to perform the necessary ceremony.

Besom weddings

If Gretna Green weddings were legal there were other unofficial rituals that were performed by couples, which – although recognised by a local community – had no official sanction. In some parts of Great Britain a 'besom wedding' was a form of temporary or trial marriage that could be undone within a year if the couple found that they were incompatible. The besom wedding was looked upon as a legal and proper marriage by the couple's community and had all the rights and obligations associated with an official wedding.

A besom is a broom or brush made from twigs or bushy plants attached to a long, stout handle (the type of broomstick that cartoon witches are popularly depicted riding). In Wales the besom wedding involved each of the couple having to jump over a broom laid across the doorway of either the groom's or bride's home – or else the couple's prospective home – without touching the door frame and before witnesses. The woman may then be given a wedding ring to wear.

If within a year the partnership does not work out through incompatibility or infertility, the unhappy partner can undo the 'marriage' by jumping backwards over a broom laid across the doorway, as before without touching the door frame and again, in front of witnesses. The couple would be considered as single and the woman as either a widow or virgin and were free to marry again. If there was a child from the 'marriage' then the father would take care of it.

In some parts of the country the expression to 'wed over a broomstick' or to be married 'over t' brush' was commonly used for a hasty or irregular marriage.

There was also a tradition from a Romany gypsy marriage ceremony whereby the couple hold hands and jump a besom made from gorse or flowering thorn, witnessed by members of their families. This was not a form of trial marriage – such a thing would be anathema to gypsy tradition and morals.

Why a broom or besom should be used for such a ceremony is not clear although it may be emblematic of the home and hearth and by extension family and family life. However, this does not really explain the Irish tradition of throwing a besom after the departing matchmaker, or anyone going on an important mission, to bring them luck.

Penny weddings

In a book entitled *The Famous History of Sir Billy of Billericay*, published in 1687, there is an account of a 'penny wedding', sometimes known as a 'beggar's wedding' or a 'public bridal':

> Now in most parts of Essex (where the wedding was kept) it is the common custom when poor people marry to make a kind of dog hanging, or money gathering, which they call a wedding dinner, to which they invite rag and tag, all that will come; where after dinner, upon the summons of a fiddler, who setteth forth his voice like a town crier, a table being set forth, and the bride set simpering at the upper end of it, the bridegroom standing by with a white sheet overthwart his shoulders, as if he did penance for the folly he had committed that day; whilst the people invited to it, like soldiers of a country train band march up to the bride, present their money and wheel about. After this offering is over there is a pair of gloves laid on the table, most monstrously bedaubed about with ribbons, which by way of auction, is set to sale, at who gives most, and he whose lot it is to have them shall withall have a kiss of the bride.

This was a way for the community to help the couple set up home in much the same way that the guests at a contemporary wedding give wedding presents to the couple.

In Cumbria these events were known as 'bridewain'; originally the word 'bridewain' referred to the wagon that transported the bride's possessions to her new home. During the journey people would make donations of goods for her new home. In time the bridewain became a collection taken by the bride, with a pewter dish on her knee, from the guests at the wedding. (The main difference between this event and the Welsh bidding tradition was that there appear to have been no meticulous accounts kept of the gifts so that they could be reciprocated.)

The penny wedding would normally be arranged by the family or some other member of the community. If the couple were in service it was not unusual for their employer to arrange a fund-raising event. On 15 November 1660, the diarist Samuel Pepys recorded attending such an event:

> To Sir W. Battens to dinner, he having a couple of servants married today; and so there was a great number of merchants, and others of good quality, on purpose after dinner to make an offering, which, when dinner was done, we did, and I did give ten shillings and no more, though I believe most of the rest did give more, and did believe that I did too.

This custom was widespread, as suggested by a letter in 1754 from a 'Gentleman in the North of Scotland':

> They have a Penny Wedding, that is, when a Servant-Maid has served faithfully, and gained good Will of her Master and Mistress they invite Relations and Friends, and there is a Dinner and Supper on the Day the Servant is married, and Musick and Dancing follow to complete the evening.
> The Bride must go about the Room and kiss every Man in the Company, and in the End every Body puts Money into a Dish. According to their Inclination and Ability.

Before the seventeenth century it was not unusual for there to be a 'wedding house' associated with the church, which had a room for the wedding feast – some had a bedchamber with a 'bridal bed' too. These wedding houses were used for penny weddings; however, some authorities disapproved of the penny wedding and attempted to suppress them, claiming that they led to disorder and licentiousness. The amounts collected could be substantial, even up to half a year's wages; this money was used to pay for the food, drink and music for the celebrations as well as helping the couple to begin their married life.

Gloves

In the account of the penny wedding from *The Famous History of Sir Billy of Billericay* there is mention of the auctioning of a pair of ribbon-decorated gloves. Gloves were traditionally given to the guests at weddings, in much the same way sugared almonds are now often given to the guests at contemporary weddings (a practice derived from Greek wedding traditions) and were, indeed, a sign of a wedding celebration. In Ben Jonson's 1609 play *The Silent Woman* one of the characters remarks:

> I see no ensigns of a wedding here, no character of a brideale
> – Where be our scarves and our gloves?

Similarly, the seventeenth-century clergyman poet Robert Herrick wrote in 'To the Maids to walk abroad':

> And talke of Brides; and who shall make
> That wedding-smock; this Bridal-Cake;
> That Dress, this Sprig, that Leaf this Vine …
> What Poses for our Wedding Rings;
> What Gloves we'l give, and Ribanings.

('Poses': a line of poetry which would be inscribed on the inside of the wedding ring.)

The number of gloves distributed at a wedding could be considerable. At the wedding of a merchant named Henry Machyn in 1560 one hundred pairs of gloves were distributed. A handwritten list headed 'gloves given at our wedding January 26th 1748' (the

A list of gloves given at a wedding, dated 1748. The bride and groom and location are unknown. (Author's collection)

name of the couple and the location of the wedding are not noted) gives the names of fifty-two people who together were given eighty-three pairs of gloves.

In his weekly journal *All the Year Round* Charles Dickens gave an account of a wedding in Wrexham in 1785 where the houses in the street where the bridegroom lived were decorated with boughs cut from trees and with ribbons and white paper cut to the shape of women's gloves.

Gloves were a common gift among friends and may have some symbolism of extending the hand of friendship. They were given as a sign of affection – if a young man gave a young woman a pair of gloves on Easter Eve and she wore them to church the next day then that was a good sign for their courtship. However, to some people the gift of gloves was considered to have the effect of breaking a friendship; some believed this could be alleviated by a token payment for the gloves.

Confetti

If gloves were the sign of a wedding in the seventeenth century, in the twentieth century the presence of coloured paper confetti signifies that a wedding has taken place. However, confetti did not become commonly used in British weddings until the late nineteenth century when it began to replace rice scattered over the bridal couple. Rice itself was a nineteenth-century introduction; in his book *Brides and Bridals*, John Cordy Jeaffreson (1872) notes:

> My friend Mr. Moncure Conway, tells me that not long since he was present at a wedding in London where rice was poured over the head of the bride. The groom and bride of this wedding were English people, moving in the middle rank of prosperous London.

This suggests that rice was recently introduced into English weddings but seems to have become firmly established a few years later. In 1880 the folklorist T. F. Thiselton-Dyer wrote that rice was scattered over the heads of the bridal couple as they left the bride's home to promote and wish them success and happiness in their future life together.

Wheat was previously scattered over the bridal couple. In his poem 'A Nuptiall Song' published in 1648 Robert Herrick has the line:

> While some repeat
> Your praise, and bless you, sprinkling you with wheat:

The obvious symbolism – that of fertility and prosperity for their married life – is reinforced by the writer Thomas Moffet who in the book *Health Improvements* (1665) noted:

> The English, when the bride comes from church, are wont to cast wheat on her head: and when the bride and bridegroom return home, one presents them with a pot of butter, as presaging plenty, and abundance of all good things.

Confetti today consists of coloured paper, good luck charm shapes, such as horseshoes or rose-petal shapes – the latter harking back to upper- or landed-class weddings where rose petals would be scattered before the bride and groom as they processed from the church. Originally confetti was small sweets (bon-bons) or paper or plaster imitations scattered during carnivals in Italy. These evolved into the paper discs or shapes used today.

In 1909 a patent application was lodged with the Patent Office in London for a cornucopia device for holding and scattering confetti at weddings and other events. The patent application explained:

> The object of this invention is to provide a combination of luck or love charms or tokens, amulets and such like, particularly in combination with a cornucopia or horn-of-plenty with Cupid embellishments, mainly for use at weddings, or other functions or events.

It is not known if any were actually produced or, if so, any survive.

Church porch weddings

Chaucer's 'Wife of Bath's Tale' in his *Canterbury Tales* reads:

> She was a worthy woman all her live,
> Husbands at the church-dore she had five.

And there is the saying, 'Happy the Bride the sun shines on; woe to the bride that the rain rains on.' Putting aside the universal wish for a sunny day for the wedding, it was not until the mid-sixteenth century that weddings were permitted in the church; the ceremony would take place in the church porch – a very public place and a place where public announcements and transactions, such as the payment of rents and bequests, took place. Until 1439 marriage was not a church sacrament and it was not until 1563 that the Catholic Church required a priest to be present for a marriage to be valid.

The *Sarum Missal*, the book of words for various services produced by Salisbury (Sarum) Cathedral, gives wording and instructions for the performance of the ceremony before the church door. The priest standing before the church door would announce the banns thrice; the woman was given by her father or her friends, with her hand uncovered (if she was a widow her hand would be covered – perhaps there is a link here with the giving of gloves and gloves being a sign of a wedding). The man makes his vows: 'I [name], take thee [name], to my wedded wife, to have and to hold from this day forward, for better for worse, for richer for poorer, in sickness and health, till death us depart, if Holy Church will it ordain, and thereto I plight thee my troth.'

The woman makes a similar oath but promises 'to be boner and buxom in bed and at board till death us depart'. The priest then blesses the ring, sprinkling it with holy water and returning it to the man to put on the three fingers and the thumb in turn with the words 'In the name of the Father, Son and Holy Ghost. Amen.' After prayers the whole company would then go into the church for a blessing.

Mass weddings

The wedding is usually a very personal affair for the couple involved and the concept of a mass or multiple wedding is usually thought of in conjunction with the Unification Church (or 'Moonies'), with thousands of couples being married in a stadium in Seoul, Korea. Mass weddings have also taken place in Iraq (in 2002 to celebrate the then president's new term of office), Kuwait, the United Arab Emirates and India to keep down the costs of dowries and the wedding celebrations especially for poorer couples. However, mass marriages on a much smaller scale were not unknown in England during the nineteenth and early twentieth centuries. They were held by the Church of England in an effort to get couples who had set up home together without the formality of a marriage to conform. A high incidence of cohabitation and common-law marriages especially in urban areas was one of the consequences of the Industrial Revolution. Mayhew in his *London Labour and London Poor* (1861–2) noted that the costermongers disliked having to pay a fee to the parson for a wedding so would only get married if it was free.

Church records from parishes in the East End of London recorded that many mass weddings were held. The Reverend Arthur W. Jepherson of St John's Church Walworth in London often carried out mass weddings sometimes marrying forty couples together. A 1903 photograph of five couples being married at the same time at St John's Church, Hoxton shows that the practice continued into the twentieth century.

A description of a mass wedding in Manchester around 1840 noted that the couples were all poor people and that since few of the brides and grooms were specially dressed for the occasion it was difficult to distinguish them from their friends and relatives. There is also a story concerning a clergyman who officiated at a mass wedding who accidentally married the wrong couples – he just told them to 'Pair as you go out; you're all married; pair as you go out.'

However, for many in the poorer parts of society a wedding was too expensive and it was not unusual for a couple to attend a marriage, follow the responses and thereby be surreptitiously married by clergy in a church. This would not be recognised as a proper marriage in law as the vows should be exchanged in front of witnesses.

Attendants

A Suffolk clergyman correspondent to Robert Chambers' *The Book of Days* (1863) said that the attendants accompanying the couple at a labourer's wedding were only three: 'the official father, the bridesmaid and the groomsman, the latter being, if possible, an engaged couple, who purpose to be the next pair to come up to the altar on a similar errand upon their own account'.

The groomsman, otherwise known now as the Best Man, whose role today is to ensure that the wedding day runs smoothly, is supposed to be the bridegroom's closest companion. His presence by the bridegroom's side is sometimes said to originate from the times of 'marriage by capture'. However, the role of the groomsman seems to have been to support the groom, act as a witness to the wedding and in some traditions, to escort the bride to the church.

The term 'Best Man' does not appear to have become common usage until the nineteenth century. Traditionally he should be unmarried; when Charles Dickens chose his publisher, John Macrone, to be his best man his fiancée objected because Macrone was a married man. Such traditions have now disappeared so that it is not unknown for a groom to have a female 'Best Man'.

The bridesmaid(s) similarly are there to support the bride but their presence is also said to be derived from 'marriage by capture, and were originally members of the groom's family who escorted her to the wedding, ensuring that she did not escape. Others have suggested that the origin of the bridesmaids is from Anglo-Saxon times when apparently the bride was led to church by a matron known as the 'brides-woman' and followed by a group of young women known as bridesmaids. Another suggested origin of the bridesmaids is that they act as doubles for the bride to protect her from malevolent influences, the evil eye and bad luck by confusing the sources of such bad wishes as to which woman was the target.

Whatever the origin, the role of the bridesmaids was, and is, to support the bride, help her get dressed and changed later on, hold her bouquet and generally assist and help the bride during the wedding. Like the Best Man the bridesmaids should be unmarried although a married woman could act as a chief bridesmaid or 'Matron of Honour'. During her duties in helping the bride remove her bridal gown the bridesmaid should ensure that all the pins used in securing the dress and bridal chaplet are removed and discarded. If the bridesmaid retains even one of the pins then she would not be married before the next Whitsuntide and if the bride accidentally, or purposely, retained one of the pins, nothing would go right for her.

Barring the way

When the bride and groom emerge from the church there was a tradition, sometimes still observed, for members of the community, usually children, to bar the way of the wedding party by tying up or obstructing the church gates or else holding a token barrier across the path. The bridegroom has to give money to the people at the barrier for the barrier to be removed and the party can continue on its way.

As the wedding usually takes place in the bride's parish this is probably a way for the bridegroom to pay his way into the community and also signal to the community that they were indeed married –

'Barring the way' in Hayton, Cumberland. (A. Bull)

important at a time when there were no photographs to capture the fact of the marriage and when the population was largely illiterate.

In 1973 Mary Huddleston gave an account of a barring the way event at a wedding in Kildwick Church, Yorkshire, where the choirboys usually tied up the church gates. On the occasion of the organist's daughter's wedding, the organist, who had not actually seen the custom before, paid the toll to the choirboys. This was proof-positive to one of the choirboys that the organist-father was the groom despite having been present throughout the wedding ceremony.

In Dungannon, Co. Tyrone, sometimes the local youths would bar the way for the bride entering the church. Similarly, in Wales the bridegroom's party would process to the bride's house to collect her and her party and then together process to the church for the wedding. It was the custom for the members of the bride's family to put barriers of straw ropes and other obstacles across the road to obstruct the groom's progress. However, there seems to be little evidence that the groom and his followers had to pay a toll at each of these barriers.

There are similar barring the way customs in countries such as Vietnam, Thailand and Germany, where the road would be barred by the young men of a village preventing the couple travelling to the church; the groom had to pay a toll before they were allowed to pass. In modern Germany the road may be barricaded by the local children as the couple leave the church after the wedding ceremony; they would be paid with money and sweets.

The scattering of money to local children after a wedding was a widespread custom, as was the common 'joke' of heating the coins before tossing them to the crowd. In the Orkney Isles, and other parts of Scotland, the bridegroom would have to contribute either a football or money for a ball to the local youths and scholars. Children would often demand the money for a ball, or 'ba'siller' (Ball Silver) outside a wedding. Mass football games were sometimes played after a wedding as were other sports.

Petting stone

Another obstacle that a bride may encounter when leaving the church is a 'petting stone' or a barrier which she must cross. Sometimes the whole congregation would have to cross the stone or barrier too. This custom seems to be prevalent in the north of England; the petting stone was often improvised and may be composed of three upright stone flags set on edge with a fourth laid flat across the top, although it could sometimes be just a stool or bench. The bride would have to either jump the barrier or stride from one end of the stone to the other, as described by John Brand in his *Observations on the Popular Antiquities of Great Britain* (1777) from Holy Island, Co. Durham:

> Whenever a marriage is solemnised at the church, after the ceremony, the bride is to step upon it, and if she cannot stride to the end thereof, it is said that the marriage will prove unfortunate.

If the bride should be reluctant or have difficulty undertaking the task, or should stumble or fall whilst leaping or stepping over the barrier then that would suggest that the marriage would be difficult. It is not mentioned what is augured if the groom should stumble.

T. F. Thiselton-Dyer in his *Church Lore Gleanings* (1891) describes an account from a wedding in 1868 where the petting stone was improvised by the wedding party:

> It was proposed to have a petted stone. A stick was therefore held by two groomsmen at the church door for the bride to jump over.

Sometimes to ensure that the bride safely negotiated the barrier she would be lifted over the stone by two men, the groom following after her and then rewarding the 'bride-lifters' with a coin. In this case etiquette suggested that she should show some reluctance to jump over the stone, displaying an appropriate modesty (which is at odds with some petting stone traditions) – if she was too eager to jump then that would be interpreted as displaying too much independence.

A tradition at Belford, Northumberland was for a stool to be put at the church door as a barrier; once the bride had leaped over the stool, complimentary verses about the bride and groom were recited. This was referred to as 'saying the noning'; the reciter or 'noning sayer' was rewarded with a silver coin.

As with many wedding customs it is difficult to provide an origin or definitive reason for the practice. Some suggest that it represents the woman leaving all her 'pets and humours' behind her, leaving her youthful obstinacies and becoming a dutiful and obedient wife (a very Victorian interpretation) whilst others have suggested, more positively, that it represents a leap forward into a new life for the newly weds.

Racing and other sports

Racing and other sports are not generally associated with a wedding but horse and running races, usually for a bride's favour or ribbon, were traditional after a wedding.

The Reverend Atkinson, writing in his memoirs in 1841 (*Forty Years in a Moorland Parish*), described a custom where after the wedding service members of the congregation in his church in

Danby-in-Cleveland, North Yorkshire, would take part in running races in the field adjoining the church for prizes of ribbons given by the bride. Atkinson notes that before he arrived at the parish the race would have been on horseback to the bride's house where the first to arrive would be presented with a ribbon. In an account of a similar race from Hornsea, East Yorkshire, in 1848 the races were run after the wedding party arrived back at the bride's house and the winner was presented with a ribbon which he wore in his hat; in later years the prize was a scarf or handkerchief.

In parts of North Yorkshire the race began as soon as the wedding ring was placed on the bride's finger. The young men would race to the bride's house with the winner having the right to remove the bride's garter from her leg. There are similar customs to this where there was a scramble for the right to remove the bride's garter, sometimes immediately after the wedding ceremony, the winner parading it round the church (to prevent herself being hurt in the scramble the bride would often have a spare garter in her bosom to give out).

William Henderson in his book *Notes on the Folklore of the Northern Counties of England and the Borders* (1866) reported that at Melsonby, near Darlington, County Durham, the bride would act as the winning post in the race, holding a ribbon in her hand – the winner receiving the ribbon and a kiss from the bride. He also recounts a case of a bride, a Methodist, who refused to provide ribbons for the races, and was ostracised by the local youths who 'fired the anvil' at her. However, it is possible that Henderson misunderstood the anvil firing, as this was usually a means of honouring and acknowledging the wedding party. In much the same way, in many Muslim countries guns are fired into the air to mark a wedding and on the continent and in Ireland horns are sounded by car drivers when driving from the church to the wedding party.

In the north-east of Scotland the race was known as 'racing for the kail'. When the wedding party came within sight of the house where the reception was to be held, the unmarried would race to 'win the kail'; it is not clear whether or not the winner received any prize but it was thought that he or she would be the first in the party to be married.

A variant of this from Ireland seemed to combine not only the sporting element but also a communal celebration. The winner of the race to the bride's house was presented with a bottle of whisky which was passed to the bridegroom, who took a drink, who then passed it to his bride, who took a drink, and then to each of the company, who each took a drink but leaving a little in the bottom of the bottle, which would be thrown away by the bridegroom.

Ribbons and favours

Today the bride's wedding car is usually decorated with white ribbons on the bonnet and door handles and male members of the wedding party wear a flower – usually a white carnation – in the buttonhole of their jacket. This is a continuation of a very long tradition of decoration with, and distribution of, ribbons and 'favours' to the wedding party and to people who could not attend the wedding.

The diarist Samuel Pepys complained in his diary entries of between 15 and 22 February 1667 that, despite loaning kitchen equipment to his colleague at the Admiralty, Sir William Penn, to help prepare the wedding dinner, he did not receive his wedding

favour until a couple of days after the wedding and after Penn had distributed them around the town. Pepys reluctantly wore the favour on his hat as was the custom.

The favour was a ribbon tied with a 'true-lovers' knot, sometimes called 'points' (a tie on the young men's hats) or 'bride-laces' (ribbons),

Sugared almonds and commercial, specially produced Love Hearts given to guests at contemporary weddings. (Author's collection)

which were distributed to the wedding guests; sometimes the ribbons would be cut up and distributed as favours. It was not just the guests who received the favours – they could be distributed to friends, family, acquaintances and servants unable to attend the wedding.

Francis Misson, a French Protestant traveller in England in the seventeenth century, was quite disparaging of the custom and that it continued amongst the English nobility, stating that in France this practice had fallen out of fashion and was only followed by the peasantry, but it had been customary to distribute a ribbon knot to be worn on the arm of the guests. He noted that the distribution of favours was not confined to the guests at a wedding but that they were given out to 'five hundred people besides'.

The distribution and wearing of the favours continued into the nineteenth century in Britain. In 1840 Sir George Head, describing a multiple wedding in a poor area of Manchester during the first half of the nineteenth century, noted that one couple arrived by horse-drawn carriage with the coachman and his companion wearing a white favour.

It was usual at this time for the bridesmaids to pin a white favour to the lapel of the groomsmen and for the men to pin them to the bodices of the bridesmaids. In parts of Scotland it was usual practice for the bride to pin a favour to the minister's sleeve after the wedding and for the bride and her 'best maid' to pin a favour to the arm of their dancing partners at the celebrations.

The flower buttonhole, the bags of sugared almonds (borrowed from Greek wedding tradition), other small gifts and, in continental Europe, the tying of a ribbon bow to car aerials (and often left for several weeks after the wedding) are all part of the continuation of a tradition of distributing wedding favours.

Walking on gold

The bride should also have a silver or gold coin in her shoe to bring luck and ensure the couple's future wealth. At one time the coin would have been a gold sovereign so that she would be 'walking on gold'. However, often a 'half-crown' coin would be used so that she would be 'walking on silver'. The Reverend Walter Gregor writing in 1881 on the folklore of north-east Scotland noted that the brides in some fishing communities would put a sixpence or shilling coin in their stocking or shoe – both silver-coloured coins. It is not the value of the coin which is important but the colour, silver or gold. Whatever the colour, the symbolism of walking on a 'precious metal' ensures future wealth.

Jewish weddings

Weddings amongst the Jewish community were exempt from the provisions of Lord Hardwick's Marriage Act (1754) because of the recognition of the separate faith of the Jews and perhaps because they were more likely to marry within their faith and there is more scrutiny of the arrangement. There is also less likelihood of clandestine marriages and marriages to separate heiresses (usually) from their fortunes because the initial arrangements are likely to have been made by a matchmaker and an essential part of the wedding ceremony is the production and reading of the *ketubah*, the marriage contract.

A parchment *ketubah* recording the marriage on Wednesday 30th Shebat which is Rosh Hodesh first Adar 5592 (1832), of David ben Asher Levi Anshul to Sarah daughter of Yehuda Leib, in London. (Jewish Museum, London)

There are nine elements to a Jewish wedding ceremony. Before the ceremony begins the groom will read the *ketubah*, which outlines the duties and responsibilities of the husband and is intended to protect the rights of the woman in the partnership and to make divorce difficult. Amongst the Jewish community this contract is important legally, more important than the wedding ring, and in Jewish law the couple could not live together without the *ketubah*. By accepting the contract the groom agrees that the rabbi can read the contract to the bride later in the ceremony.

The veiling of the bride, *bedeken*, recalls the biblical story where Jacob was tricked into marrying Leah instead of her younger sister Rachel as promised. *Bedeken* means to check; the groom is escorted to the bride's room and by lifting the veil checks to confirm that the bride is the right woman. When the veil has been lifted the rabbi blesses the bride and then the couple are escorted to the *huppah*.

The *huppah*, or canopy, is said to represent the new home, open on all four sides to symbolise hospitality. Although the canopy is usually associated with the Jewish wedding ceremony it does not seem to have been introduced until the sixteenth century, and then with reluctance. It is believed that a form of canopy was used in weddings in the British Isles during the fourteenth century and earlier and is found in a number of traditions worldwide. In Sri Lanka, for example, a canopy is used and it is also used in Hindu and Jain weddings.

Despite the solemnity of the occasion there is sometimes a little bit of 'power play' beneath the *huppah*. If the man puts his right foot on the bride's left foot during the blessing he will have authority over her during the marriage; however, if she manages to put her left foot on his right, then she will have authority.

Under the *huppah* the bride makes seven circuits around the groom, representing the seven days of creation and to remind the couple that marriage is a re-enactment of the creative process and that the couple are creating a new life together and becoming a new unit in the community.

The next stage is the betrothal ceremony, the *kudushin*, where the bride and groom sip wine from a cup to remind them that from now on they will share the same 'cup of life'. The rabbi will recite two betrothal blessings and the groom says, in Hebrew, 'You are now consecrated to me with this ring according to the law of Moses and Israel' and he places the ring on the index finger of her right hand.

Jewish wedding rings, from *Finger-Ring Lore* by William Jones, published in 1898.

Many of the wedding rings traditionally used are very elaborate; some designs have a building on the bezel of the ring symbolising the Temple and the home.

After the placing of the ring the *ketubah* is read out in Aramaic – with a translation.

The betrothal ceremony over the marriage ceremony, *nissuin*, follows with seven blessings recited over a cup of wine to seal the union. The end of this part of the ceremony is marked by the groom crushing the wine glass beneath the heel of his shoe, said to symbolise the destruction of the Temple in Jerusalem and to remind the couple of the sorrows of Israel. This act is sometimes interpreted as being to ward off evil spirits. When the glass is crushed the congregation shout '*mazal tov*' ('good fortune') and then the rabbi blesses the couple.

The legal aspect of the marriage is the signing of the civil register before two witnesses; the couple are then given the *ketubah* and their state marriage certificate. The couple then retire to the bride's room where they have a moment of privacy, known as the *yichud*, and break their fast.

After the wedding ceremony money may be scattered amongst the crowd and barley or confetti may be scattered over the couple to wish them many children.

Quaker weddings

The other religious group exempt from Lord Hardwick's Marriage Act were the Quakers, or Religious Society of Friends. The Quakers do not believe that there is a need for clergy to act as intermediaries between man and God and therefore have no clergy but do have a system of elders who may lead worship.

A Quaker wedding is very like Quaker worship. There is no formal procession, division between families or order of worship. As with their meetings for worship, the meeting is silent – the bride and groom and the meeting sitting in contemplation but those present are invited to contribute their thoughts, a special poem, readings and wishes as they feel moved.

When they are ready the couple will stand and make their vows before the meeting and a registrar – it is necessary for a registrar to be present for the marriage to be legal. There is a form of template for the vows but the couple can customise the vows to themselves.

After the vows the couple may exchange rings and resume their seats in the meeting. Towards the end of the meeting, judged by the elders, the couple and the chief witnesses sign a Quaker certificate which is read out to the meeting. After the meeting has finished all those present sign the certificate as witnesses.

Until 1872 the Quakers had a system of preliminary investigation before a marriage could take place. The couple would have to declare their intention to marry at the bride-to-be's meeting. The meeting would then appoint members to investigate and report on whether there were any impediments to the marriage. The following month the couple would have to declare their intention for a second time, and, if the reports found nothing wrong, they were told that they could go ahead with the marriage.

After 1872 the law required that a notice of intention to marry had to be posted in the office of the superintendent registrar (equivalent to publishing the banns of marriage) and this provided enough of a safeguard against clandestine or irregular marriages.

Recording the day

It is now customary to have a complete photographic and video record of the wedding day, which can later be shown to those who attended the event and those unable to attend alike. However, photography did not become an integral part of the wedding ceremonial until well into the twentieth century.

Photography developed around 1830 so it was only the wealthy and fashionable who could afford to have a photograph taken of the wedding and by the end of the century a photographer could be engaged for the day.

During the first part of the twentieth century a visit to the photographer's studio was within the reach of many people of all classes and this became part of the recording of the marriage. The couple and other members of the wedding party would go to the photographer's studio in their wedding clothes, a few days after the marriage, for the wedding photographs.

Towards the middle of the century photography became quicker so the bridal party would often call into the photographer's studio on their way to the wedding reception. However, by around the 1950s photographic equipment was becoming more portable and it became feasible and more popular to hire a photographer to attend the wedding and record more of the event. Many new conventions have arisen following this development, such as the nature of group shots, and who stands where and next to whom. In recent years, a greater prevalence of divorce and re-marriage has created its own complications.

Wedding-day luck

Because a wedding is a life-changing event there are many superstitions and auguries of good and bad luck surrounding the day, the preparations and the celebrations of the marriage, many of which have already been mentioned or will be mentioned in the next section. Brides often carry small amulets such as silver-coloured card horseshoes and black cats to bring good luck.

Good luck wedding arch, Wales. (Collections Picture Library)

The black cat appears to be luck bringing in the context of a wedding. In some areas it is said that if there is a black cat in the house then the girls will not be short of suitors. If a bride hears a black cat sneeze on her wedding day she will be happy throughout her married life and if she sees a black cat on her way to, or as she is leaving the church after the ceremony, she will have a prosperous and happy marriage. On the negative side it is considered unlucky for the bridal party to meet a funeral on the way to the church.

There were a few churches that were considered to endow good fortune for those marrying in them. The church of All Saints at Rayne, Essex was said to bring good luck. The legend runs that during the fourteenth century the mistress of a farmhouse called Nailinghurst was in labour and it was not going well. The maids were sent to the church to pray to the Virgin Mary for their mistress. As they prayed a vision of the Virgin Mary appeared to them, smiled upon them and then vanished. When they returned to the house they found their mistress had been safely delivered of her child.

A similar legend from the thirteenth century surrounds the church at Ashingdon, Essex, where the image of the Virgin Mary was said to have the power to help barren women. Hundreds of pilgrims would crawl on their knees to the church where they made an offering to the Virgin Mary. The rector became a wealthy man from all the pilgrims but this caused the local clergy to complain to the Bishop of London who discouraged and suppressed the pilgrimages in 1304. However, the church became known to be propitious for marriage because of a belief that couples marrying there would be blessed with children.

In Suffolk couples avoid passing over the Goldbrook Bridge on the road between the villages of Hoxne and Cross Street, Suffolk, to get to the church for their wedding. The story goes that King Edmund was running away from the Danes and hid under the bridge; however, he was betrayed by a newly wed couple returning home in the evening who saw his spurs reflected in the water in the moonlight, so Edmund laid a curse on any couple who crossed the bridge on their way to their wedding.

The Goldbrook Bridge, Hoxne, Suffolk. It was believed that couples crossing this bridge on the way to their wedding would be cursed. (Collections Picture Library)

CELEBRATIONS

The wedding breakfast

A feast and celebration after the wedding itself is an almost universal event; in the British Isles this is generally a very formal event which in the nineteenth century became known as the 'wedding breakfast'.

From 1604 canonical law stated that marriages could only take place between the hours of eight o'clock in the morning and midday, unless a special licence was obtained. Marriages anyway had to take

'A Weddynge Breakfaste', a line drawing from *Manners and Customs of Ye Englyshe in 1849.* (Collections Picture Library)

place during daylight hours but it was not until 1934 that marriages were allowed in the afternoon, but not after 6 p.m.

Amongst the Victorian genteel classes it became the fashion to have a 'breakfast' after the ceremony; this could be anything from a light buffet to a full-blown meal. As with many aspects of the 'traditional' British wedding the aspiring middle and lower classes in an effort to appear fashionable absorbed this practice, which also became embedded in wedding etiquette books.

A 1932 book, *The Bride's Book or Young Housewife's Compendium*, by 'Two Ladies of England', drew a distinction between the wedding breakfast – a formal affair with toasts and speeches – and an afternoon tea reception which was informal and no speeches were given or formal and public toasts proposed.

But the wedding feast has always been a feature of weddings and, before the seventeenth century, many churches and philanthropists provided a wedding house with a room for the celebrations, such as the marriage feast room at Matching, Essex, provided by one William Chimney in 1480. Often a bedchamber with a bridal bed would also be provided.

Hot pot

During the reception the guests toast the bride and groom (and the bridesmaids) – to wish them good fortune and good health. There were, however, other customs in which the community would wish the couple good fortune. One such, which was practised at least until the end of the nineteenth century, was the preparation of a drink known as 'hot pot'. This was a concoction of spiced and sweetened ale prepared by the friends and neighbours of the bridal couple.

The bridal party were expected to have a taste of the hot pot at each house they passed on their journey from the church after the wedding; the wedding party could have drunk a considerable amount of spiced ale before they arrived home. In some places it was the practice for the makers of the hot pots to take the brew to the church to meet the bridal party. In *The Knot Tied: Marriage Customs of all Nations* (1877) William Tegg described the custom as encountered by a correspondent:

> ... the bridal party having formed in procession for leaving
> the church, we were stopped in the porch by a row of five or
> six women, ranged to our left hand, each holding a large mug
> with a cloth over it. These were in turn presented to me, and
> handed by me to my wife, who, after taking a sip, returned it
> to me. It was then passed to the next couple, and so on in the
> same form to all the party. The composition in these mugs
> was, mostly, I am sorry to say, simply horrible; one or two were
> very fair, one very good. They were sent to the church by all
> classes, and are considered a great compliment.

The Tegg correspondent mentioned the variable nature of the
offerings, which was not unusual; other descriptions of the custom
remark that the hot pots were '... of quality according to his
ability...'.

It was considered an unlucky omen if any of the spiced ale from
the first bowl were to be accidentally spilt because the couple would
have let slip the first kindly wishes for their health and happiness.

Hot pot is reminiscent of a traditional bedtime drink known as
'posset', or 'sack posset', which, in the seventeenth century, was a
mixture of milk, wine, egg yolk, sugar, cinnamon, nutmeg and other
spices. The posset appears to have been quite a thick mixture, as the
antiquarian John Brand wrote in 1777:

> In the evening of the wedding day, immediately before
> retirement of the company, Sack Posset was eaten, the bride
> and the groom tasting it first; and this was given the name of
> Benediction Posset.

Catholic couples would be blessed by the priest as they sat on the
bridal bed, wearing their best dressing gowns and surrounded by their
closest friends; the priest also blessed the bed and a cup of sweetened
and spiced liquor known as the benediction posset. When the posset
had been drunk the friends dispersed and the bed curtains were drawn.

Jeaffreson's (1872) description of the posset is of a concoction of
'beer and plum buns – cakes swimming in a bowl of spiced ale',

which he says was 'forced' upon the bride as she entered the bridal chamber, 'in the belief that no other combination of food and drink was so calculated to restore the exhausted energies of a delicate young lady'.

There was a divination game played using the posset where a wedding ring was dropped into the mixture and the posset distributed amongst the unmarried people. The person finding the ring would be the next to be married.

To bed and throwing the stockings

The consummation of the marriage is considered an important element as confirmation of the marriage and the guests would accompany the couple to bed, which obviously led to some horseplay and hilarity. An account of a wedding in Derbyshire in 1753 noted: 'the newly married couple ... were at length put to bed ... the stocking was thrown, and the whole concluded with all Decorum, Decency and order imaginable'.

The stocking throwing referred to a custom where after the bride and groom had prepared themselves for bed two of the groomsmen would sit on one side of the bed with their backs to the centre of the bed and each with one of the groom's stockings; similarly, two of the bridesmaids would sit on the other side again with their backs to the centre. Each would, in turn, throw the stocking over their shoulder, the groomsmen hoping to hit the bride and the bridesmaids hoping to hit the groom. A hit would indicate that the thrower would soon be married.

'Blessing the Nuptial Bed', 1575. From *Illustrations of Shakespeare* by Francis Douce, 1839. (Collections Picture Library)

Francis Maximilian Misson, who travelled around England in

the seventeenth-century, described the custom in his *Memoirs and Observations on His Travels over England* (1698):

> The Bridesmen take the Bride's stockings, and the Bridesmaids the Bridegroom's; Both sit down at the Bed's Feet, and fling the Stockings over their Heads, endeavouring to direct them so as that they fall upon the marry'd couple. If the Man's stocking, thrown by the Maid, fall upon the Bridegroom's Head, it is a Sign she will quickly be marry'd herself; and the same Prognostick holds good of the Woman's Stockings, thrown by the Man. Oftimes these young people engage with one another upon the Success of the Stockings, tho' they themselves look upon it to be nothing but sport.

There is a similar practice from north-east Scotland, where the bridal bed would be made up by a woman currently breast-feeding to ensure that the couple would be blessed with children, the guests would crowd into the bedroom where the bride would go to bed first, and the bridegroom would throw his stocking into the crowd. The one who caught it would be the next to marry.

Some newly wed brides would try to foretell how her life would continue by throwing a stocking over her left shoulder as she prepared for bed. If the stocking landed in a straight line her luck would be continuous; if, however, it was not straight her luck would be variable.

Bouquets and shoes

The modern equivalent of the stocking-throwing custom is for the bride to throw her bouquet to the unmarried, usually female guests – the one catching it would be the next to marry. This is probably a relatively recent addition to the canon of wedding traditions dating from the late nineteenth century, especially as the bouquet is now usually thrown as the couple leave the reception to go on their honeymoon.

The going away car is usually decorated by the friends of the couple who see them off. Sometimes the decoration can be extreme

The decorated going-away car.

and often involves tying boots and tin cans to the rear bumper. The tin cans seem obvious – as they drive away the cans make a huge noise, drawing attention to the couple, the decorated car and the fact that the occupants are newly weds.

Boots and shoes tied behind have a less obvious meaning but there is a long tradition of shoes being thrown after a person to bring them good luck. In *Great Expectations* by Charles Dickens (published 1861), the hero, Pip, leaves home to go to London:

> The last I saw of them was, when I presently heard a scuffle
> behind me, and looking back, saw Joe throw an old shoe after
> me, and Biddy throwing another old shoe.

In Ireland an old shoe would be thrown after someone going to a fair to bring them luck. (Fairs were originally held for trade and exchange of labour; today's funfairs have arisen from these.)

In the Isle of Man it was usual to throw an old shoe after the bride and the groom as they left their separate homes for the church. If on the way back from the church one of the guests managed to remove one of the bride's shoes then the groom would have to pay a ransom.

William Tegg, writing in 1877, described how a newly wed couple, obviously of the moneyed class, would have to pass through a double file of friends and domestics, each of whom carried a slipper, to get to their carriage after the reception; as the carriage drew away the slippers were flung after it for good luck.

Although shoe throwing, or attaching boots and shoes to the going away car, is generally to bring luck and good fortune, there were further practices concerning shoes which have little to do with luck bringing. William Hone in his *Table Book* (1841) described a custom of 'trashing' where old shoes were thrown at a bridal couple who had not contributed to the conviviality of the local scholars. This transformed over time into indiscriminate shoe throwing as a piece of fun and sometimes with turf or clumps of mud substituted for shoes.

In Orkney it was traditional for the bridegroom to donate a football, or the money for a football, to the children of the bride's parish. If the money was not forthcoming they would claim their 'ba'money' and if the money was not paid they would take the bride's shoe.

There was also a Kentish custom where a shoe was thrown by the chief bridesmaid and other single women scrambled for the shoe; the winner of the shoe would be the next to marry. One of her shoes was then thrown at the men – the one hit by the shoe would be the first among them to be married.

Rough band, serenades and lucky visitors

In East Anglia the 'rough band' – which was usually a form of punishment for social transgressors, usually matrimonial-related offences such as wife-beating, being unfaithful or a wedding under dubious circumstances – became part of the community celebration of a marriage. The rough band consisted of a group of people banging pans and saucepans to make a terrible noise. This tradition survived in East Anglia into the twentieth century; the 'performers', on learning that there was a wedding celebration at one of the houses, would make their 'music' and give a song outside the house until they were invited inside for a drink (and some food).

In a way this has some similarities with the Irish straw boys – a group of mummers, dressed head to foot in a straw costume who would visit the wedding house and dance with all the women, the leader of the group claiming the right to dance with the bride. In County Kerry the straw boys would visit the bride's house on the eve of the wedding. Unlike the rough band, this whole event took place in silence and was thought to bring good luck and fortune to the bride and groom.

The luck-bringing stranger can also be found in the tradition that it was considered lucky for a chimney sweep, dressed in his 'blacks', or working clothes, with a blackened face, to appear at a wedding – usually after the couple have emerged from the church. Local newspapers often printed a bride being kissed on the cheek by the blackened chimney sweep. Face blacking was a traditional way to disguise luck bringers – often mummers or Morris men – but the sweep may also have had associations with hearth and home and

London Butchers' Marrowbone and Cleaver Band serenading a newly married couple. From Chambers' *Book of Days*, 1863.

there could be some relevant symbolism there. However, in the days where open fires and dirty chimneys were commonplace, and before the advent of central heating and vacuum chimney cleaning, appearing at weddings was a handy and profitable sideline for chimney sweeps. Miniature chimney sweeps are among the good luck charms sometimes given to the bride on her wedding day along with horseshoes and silver shoes.

An 'institution of the London vulgar' described by Robert Chambers in his *Book of Days* (1863) which he said was 'one just about to expire', was the Marrowbone and Cleaver Band which serenaded a newly wed couple:

> The performers were the butchers' men, – 'the bonny boys that wear the sleeves of blue.' A set of these lads, having duly accomplished themselves for the purpose, made a point of attending in front of a house containing a wedding party, with their cleavers, and each provided with a marrowbone, where with to perform a sort of rude serenade, of course with the expectation of a fee in requital of their music. Sometimes, the group would consist of four, the cleaver of each ground to the production of a certain note; but a full band – one entitled to the highest grade of reward – would be not less than eight, producing a complete octave; and, where there was a fair skill, this series of notes would have all the fine effect of a peal of bells. When this serenade happened in the evening, the men would be dressed neatly in clean blue aprons, each with a portentous wedding favour of white paper in his breast or hat. It was wonderful with what quickness and certainty, under the enticing presentiment of beer, the serenaders got wind of a coming marriage, and with what tenacity of purpose they would go on with their performance until the expected crown or half-crown was forthcoming.

Dancing in green stockings

It was expected that within a family the eldest would be married before the younger siblings – such an order has been followed or expected across many cultures and ages. In the Old Testament story of Jacob wanting to marry Rachel, the younger daughter in the family, he was told '… it is not our custom to give the younger daughter in marriage before the older one…' (Gen. 29. 26). However, if a younger sister did marry before her elder sister there was a tradition for the elder sister to dance in a hog's (pig's) trough on the wedding day. In *The Taming of the Shrew* by William Shakespeare (Act 2, scene 1) Katharina says to her father, regarding her younger sister:

> She is your treasure, she must have a husband;
> I must dance bare-foot on her wedding-day,
> And for your love to her lead apes in hell.

In some traditions she would have to dance barefoot; in others she would have to wear green stockings. The green stockings may have been a sign of shame and green is considered an unlucky colour. This may have been a demeaning act to break her bad luck.

This custom was not, however, confined to the women of the family: there is an account of a brother having to perform the dance and being so vigorous as to break the trough.

Honeymoon

The communal celebrations included a great deal of eating, drinking and even seeing the couple off to bed with a certain amount of ritual. Until recent times, the concept of going away for a 'honeymoon' was completely unknown and alien to most newly wed couples.

There are a number of myths about the honeymoon and derivation of the holiday. The term 'honeymoon' is thought to be of sixteenth-century origin and indicated a waning of affection or sweetness post marriage. Explanations include the couple drinking honey wine for thirty days after the marriage and some have suggested that this period goes back to the practice of 'marriage by capture' where the young man would keep the woman in seclusion, away from her family and friends for a period.

However, for most people the concept of going away from work for a long period was not possible. Their friends and family, and working life, would only allow enough seclusion for the relationship to be consummated (an essential part of the wedding – non-consummation of the marriage was a justification for annulment). The bridal tour, or honeymoon, did not become fashionable until the late eighteenth century, but then only for the richer stratum of society. By the beginning of the nineteenth century the fashion was set. The aristocratic and landed gentry would generally travel to the continent for a honeymoon lasting about a month. In his book *Brides and Bridals*, John Cordy Jeaffreson writing in 1872 outlined the type of honeymoon experienced by various levels of society:

> The honeymoon trip of a married couple, who though of gentle quality, were too busy or thrifty to think of spending much time or money on a romantic excursion, seldom exceed ten days or a fortnight. The London merchant or lawyer took his London bride to Bath or Tunbridge Wells or Brighton for seven or eight days … The country clergyman or provincial doctor took his spouse for a short time to London to see parks and theatres, St Paul's and the Tower …

For most people the wedding took place during a short break in their usual working day and they may have had a day off for a honeymoon if they were lucky. There are even accounts of couples going away to stay with relatives and working on the farm and in the house during their stay.

The honeymoon did not become common amongst all levels of society until around the middle of the twentieth century and was probably promoted by the increasing ease of transport.

Continuing celebrations

Not all wedding customs took place on the wedding day; a Scottish custom, called 'creeling', which died out during the nineteenth century, took place on the day after the wedding. The newly married couple and their friends met early in the morning and a creel, a type of basket, was filled with stones and fixed to the new husband's back. He had to run round the town, followed by a group of the young men who would make sure that he did not drop the creel, until his wife gave him a kiss.

In parts of Ayrshire the event happened the second day after the wedding; the couple and their friends met up and the creel was filled with stones. The young men took turns to carry the creel and allowed themselves to be caught by the women, who would give them a kiss. Finally the creel fell to the new husband who was obliged to carry the creel for a long time before his wife took pity on him, caught up with him and gave him the requisite kiss. This was proof of her satisfaction with him.

In Ireland 'show Sunday' was almost a repeat of the wedding where the bride and groom and their attendants, wearing their wedding finery, went to church the Sunday following the wedding, sitting in the pew at the front of the church and even standing up to face the congregation during the sermon. This was a form of public confirmation of the marriage. This practice declined, probably due to the increasing popularity of the honeymoon trip, but the additional recognition and celebration of the marriage took place on the couple's return with a 'hauling home' party in which neighbours and relations were invited to the house for food, drink and music.

Carrying over the threshold

The proper beginning of the newly married couple's new life together is when they enter their home together. It was therefore considered bad luck for the woman to stumble as she crossed the threshold – this was seen as an omen for an unhappy marriage; perhaps the stumble could be interpreted as an unconscious reluctance on the part of the bride to become a wife. (In some cultures the bride was expected to show a reluctance to get married, with some ritualised form of resistance to being taken to the marriage ceremony.)

This may be one of the reasons for the tradition for the groom to carry his new wife over the threshold of their new home. This tradition is also said to be derived from the Rape of the Sabine Women, described by the Roman historian Livy, which is said to be the origin of the Roman practice for the bride to be carried into the house by a group of people.

However, the threshold to the house was noted as being susceptible to malign magic and malevolent sources, which could destroy the marriage by sorcery. Ben Jonson in his *Masque of Hymen* (1606) warns the bride to step boldly over the threshold:

> Haste, tender lady, and adventure;
> The covetous house would have you enter,
> That it might wealthy be,
> And you her mistress, see:
> Haste your own good to meet;
> And lift your golden feet
> About the threshold high,
> With prosperous augury.

It was therefore important for the bride to step over the threshold without touching it so it was expedient to carry her over the threshold.

In a 'broomstick wedding', the couple had to jump over a broom laid across the doorway without touching the doorway. A method for providing protection against witches and sorcerers was to place a bowl of salt and a broom at the doorway; the witch would have to count the grains of salt and the straws in the broom before entering, a task thought impossible to achieve between the hours of midnight and dawn, so effectively protecting the house and the inhabitants.

In the seventeenth century it was customary for the new bride to be presented with the keys to the house, symbolising her becoming mistress of the house.

In north-east Scotland there was a custom of the bride being met at the doorway of her new home by two of her female friends who would put a towel over her head and pour a basket of bread over her – the bread was collected by the children. At one time she would have been led to the hearth where the fire had been scattered and she would be handed the fire tongs to make up the fire. The bread represented prosperity, whilst making up the fire in the hearth – often considered the heart of the home – made her the mistress of the home.

TOGETHER FOREVER

The Dunmow flitch

The 'Dunmow flitch' ceremony takes place every four years (leap years) in mid-June in the Essex town of Dunmow. This ceremony awards a couple who can honestly say that they have been married for a year and a day without any regrets – sleeping or waking – or ever wishing themselves unwed, with a flitch of bacon (a side of hog, salted and cured). The custom's beginnings are lost in the mists of time but it was well known at the time of Chaucer who referred to it in the 'Wife of Bath's Tale' in *The Canterbury Tales* (first published in 1387):

> The bacon was not fet him I trow,
> That some men have in Essex at Dunmow.

However, it is said that the custom was initiated by Lady Juga Baynard in around 1104 when she founded the Little Dunmow Priory to encourage people to get married in church. It is also suggested that the event was instituted by Robert Fitzwalter in the thirteenth century. In any event the awarding of the Dunmow flitch has had quite a chequered history. There are no surviving accounts of the flitch being awarded before 1445, when it was claimed by a labourer from Badbury, Norfolk, named Richard Wright. The next recorded claimant was Stephen Samuel of Ayston-Parva, Essex, who in 1467 made the required oath before the prior, Roger Bulcott, the convent and some neighbours. A third recorded claimant around this time was Thomas le Fuller from Coggeshall, Essex, who made the oath before the prior, John Tils, the convent and neighbours.

There may have been other claimants but no further claimants are recorded before 1701, when a case was examined with full scrutiny and ceremony. The court roll of Dunmow records:

> At a Court Baron of the Right Worshipful Sir Thomas May, Knight, there holden upon Friday the 7th day of June in the 13th year of the reign of our sovereign Lord William III., by the grace of God … and in the year of our Lord 1701, before Thomas Wheeler, Gent., Steward of the said Manor. It is thus enrolled
> Elizabeth Beaumont, spinster.
> Henrietta Beaumont, spinster.
> Annabella Beaumont, spinster
> Jane Beaumont, spinster.
> Mary Wheeler, spinster.

Taking the oath at Dunmow for the flitch of bacon. From Hone's *Every-day Book* 1841.

Be it remembered that at this court, in full and open court, it is found and presented … that William Parsley, of Much Easton, in the county of Essex, butcher, and Jane his wife, have been married for the space of three years past and upward; and it is likewise found, presented and adjudged by the homage aforesaid that the said William Parsley and Jane his wife … are fit and qualified persons to be admitted by the court to receive the ancient and accustomed oath, whereby to entitle themselves to have the bacon of Dunmow delivered unto them according to the custom of the manor.

The oath was administered by the steward whilst the couple knelt on two pointed stones at the church door:

> You do swear by custom of confession,
> That you ne'er made Nuptial Transgression;
> Nor since you were married man and wife,
> By household brawles or contentious strife,
> Or otherwise in bed or at boarde,
> Offended each other in Deed or in Word:
> Or in twelvemonth's time and a day,
> Repented not in any way;
> Or since the Church Clerke said Amen,
> Wished yourselves unmarried again,
> But continue true and in desire
> As when you joined hands in holy quire.

After the oath the court pronounced the sentence:

> Since to these conditions, without any fear,
> Of your own accord you do freely swear,
> A whole gammon of bacon you do receive,
> And bear it away with love and good leave:
> For this is the Custom of Dunmow well known;
> Tho' the pleasure be ours, the bacon's your own.

The description of the event in 1751 – the next recorded awarding of the flitch – is more like the present ceremony. A John Shakeshaft and his wife, from Weathersfield, Essex, appeared before the Court Baron and persuaded a jury of six bachelors and six maidens that they should receive the prize. They were paraded through the town on a chair ('chaired') with the Steward and other officers of the Manor, preceded by the flitch and watched by a crowd of (apparently) 5,000 people. John Shakeshaft made a lot of money that day selling slices of the bacon to the crowd.

The custom fell into abeyance after this, despite a couple trying to claim the flitch in 1772 – the gates of the priory were locked fast and they and their supporters had to leave empty handed – and by this time the kneeling stones were removed from the churchyard.

In 1851 another couple approached the then Lord of the Manor to claim the flitch, but he declined their request on the grounds that the custom had been dormant for so long. However, because they

THE DUNMOW PROCESSION, 1751.

Dumnow flitch ceremony, 1751. John Shakeshaft and his wife, from Weathersfield in Essex, are 'chaired' through the town with the Steward and other officers of the Manor, preceded by the flitch and watched by the crowd.

were so disappointed and their friends quite annoyed with this a compromise was reached whereby the couple received the bacon, after taking the required oath, at a nearby rural fete.

The current Dunmow flitch trial event owes its revival to the nineteenth-century popular novelist Harrison Ainsworth, after the publication of his novel *The Flitch of Bacon, or the Custom of Dunmow, a Tale of English Home Life* (1854). He was determined to revive the custom and, after being refused permission to hold the event at Little Dunmow – the original location – moved the event to Great Dunmow against opposition from some of the gentry and clergy. (Harrison Ainsworth was also responsible for romanticising Dick Turpin, who was actually a vicious criminal, and credited him with the famous ride to York actually carried out by the Highwayman 'Swiftnick' Nevison.)

Ainsworth donated two flitches and served as the first judge for the revived trial held at the Town Hall in 1855. The claimants being found worthy of the flitches, they took the oath in the nearby Windmill Field, watched by about 7,000 people.

The trials were interrupted in the twentieth century by the two world wars; the 1949 revival event was made possible only through the Commonwealth Gift Scheme because the country was still subject to rationing. However, the custom continues and takes the form of a mock trial with celebrities taking the part of counsel and with a jury of six bachelors and six spinsters. The recipients are 'chaired' through the town in triumph.

The origins of the custom are lost but writing in 1863, Robert Chambers in his *Book of Days* suggests that it began as a form of ecclesiastical joke, where the celibate monks of the Priory of Little Dunmow considered the likelihood of marital harmony existing for any length of time to be so scarce that they would offer a flitch of bacon to any couple who could swear on oath that they had not regretted their marriage nor had a cross word for a year and a day and could honestly say that they would do the same again if they had the chance.

The Little Dunmow Priory was not the only place to offer a flitch of bacon for matrimonial fidelity. Apparently the Abbey of

St Melaine, near Rennes, had a flitch of bacon hanging for more than six centuries, remaining quite fresh, for the first couple who lived together without grumbling, repenting the marriage or dispute for a year and a day.

In around 1337 the Lord of the Manor, Sir Philip de Somerville, at Wychnor, near Lichfield, Staffordshire, offered a flitch of bacon for marital fidelity. The bacon was to be laid on a bed of a quarter of wheat and a quarter of rye; the claimants would have to swear the oath whilst on one knee:

> Hear ye, Sir Philip de Somerville, lord of Whichenoure, maintain and giver of this Bacon, that I, *A*, syth I wedded *B*, my wyfe, and syth I had her in my keeping and at wylle, by a Yere and a Daye after our Marryage, I would not have changed for none other, farer ne fowler, richer ne pourer, ne for none other descended of gretter lynage, sleeping ne waking, at noo time, and if the said *B* were sole and I sole, I would take her to be my wyfe before all other wymen of the worlde, of what condytion soevere they be, good or evyle, as helpe me God, and Seyntys, and this flesh and all fleshes.

It was noted in 1780 that the flitch had remained unclaimed.

Wife selling

At the other end of the matrimonial scale if the marriage was not happy, until the early twentieth century, it was extremely difficult for a couple to get a divorce, a fact reflected in the saying 'Marry in haste, repent at leisure'. Many societies have long had a means of undoing a marriage with some form of compensation written into or as part of a marriage agreement or settlement. This was so until about the tenth century in northern Europe when church authorities imposed a marriage regime which did not allow easy divorce or re-marriage. This state of affairs continued until 1857, despite the well-known reason for the split from the Church of Rome and the establishment of the Church of England by Henry VIII – because he wanted a divorce from Catherine of Aragon. (The Archbishop of

Canterbury declared this marriage null and void, but of his other five marriages one ended in divorce in 1540.)

There were, as mentioned in previous sections, trial marriages which did not confer a lifetime obligation – but these were not sanctioned by the church, and there were cases, especially in remote areas, where couples would set up home together and travelling priests would legally marry the couple in retrospect. However, trial marriage arrangements were not legally binding in the eyes of the authorities even if believed so by the 'folk'. For those who were legally married but who could not afford to undo the marriage legally, the practice of 'wife selling', a very public act of separation, developed; this was erroneously believed to be legal and above board.

The practice seems to have developed during the seventeenth century; in *Jackson's Oxford Journal* of 12 December 1789 wife selling was described as a '… vulgar mode of *Divorce* lately adopted.' Thomas Hardy caused consternation in Victorian society when, in his novel *The Mayor of Casterbridge* (1886), a drunken husband sold his wife and child to a sailor for the sum of five guineas (£5, 5s). Although this was a well-known form of divorce for the poorer classes of society, Victorian literary society did not want what they considered a degrading practice featured in popular fiction as it gave a bad impression of British society. However, although the custom superficially appears degrading, delving deeper into the practice there is more going on.

It is worth briefly considering divorce in Great Britain before the laws were relaxed in the second half of the twentieth century. For most people divorce was almost impossible. Before the 1857 Matrimonial Causes Act, which made a civil divorce possible, a couple would have to get an act of Parliament to annul the marriage. The process was outlined by a Judge Maul in his address to a prisoner convicted of bigamy in 1855:

> You had no right to take the law into your own hands … I will
> tell you what you ought to have done. Immediately you heard
> of your wife's adultery you should have gone to an attorney
> and directed him to bring an action against the seducer of your

wife … You should have employed a proctor, and instituted a suit in the Ecclesiastical Courts for a divorce *mensa et thoro* [literally, 'by table and by bed', a form of divorce equating to what we would now term a separation]. Your case is a very clear one, and I doubt not you would have obtained your divorce. After this step your course was quite plain: you had only to obtain a private Act of Parliament to dissolve your marriage. This you would get as a matter of course, on the payment of the proper fees and proof of the facts. You might then have lawfully married again … you would tell me that these proceedings would cost you £1,000, and that your small stock-in-trade is not worth £100. Perhaps that may be so. The law has nothing to say to that. If you had taken these proceedings you would have been free from your present wife, and the woman whom you secondly married would have been a respectable matron. As you have not done so, you stand there a convicted culprit, and it is my duty to pass sentence upon you. You will be imprisoned for one day.

The 1857 Act that established the divorce courts still did not make things easy. However, given the difficulty of getting a divorce, it is not surprising that there should have been a form of 'folk' divorce and this took the form of an apparently humiliating wife sale.

The details of this varied from place to place but was quite ritualistic and, unlike Thomas Hardy's fictional wife sale, was performed completely sober and with the consent of all parties involved. Accounts of sales suggest that cash transaction was not the motive for the sale: in Stowmarket, Suffolk, in 1787 a farmer sold his wife for five guineas and then gave her a guinea to buy a new gown and ordered the bells to be rung in celebration. And a 1796 report from Sheffield, Yorkshire, recorded that a wife was sold for 6d, then the husband paid a guinea for a coach to take her and her purchaser to Manchester.

The ritual usually involved the husband leading his wife to market with a halter of rope, straw or ribbon round her neck. In Warwickshire the husband would have to lead her through three toll gates, paying a toll at each turnpike, or through three villages on the road to the market place. At the market the husband or the Town Crier would announce her good and bad points and then she would be 'sold' to the highest bidder.

Whilst this whole ritual appears humiliating for the wife, it was also humiliating for the husband who was publicly admitting the failure of the marriage and the fact that he had been 'cuckolded'. It was not unusual for the husband to wear horns on his head – the sign of being cuckolded – as he led his wife to the sale site.

The bidder was often known to the woman and was considered a way of getting out of an unhappy or unsatisfactory marriage. Sometimes the woman would supply the money to an agent or even her own brothers to bid for her.

It would seem that it was more usual for her to be bought by a lover; in a number of accounts, a purchaser was from the couple's village, who happened to be in the market on the right day and at the right time. Sometimes the wife sale could be seen to solve a problem in the times of difficult communications – when a husband would go off to war, for example, and be away for a very long time with no word getting back to his wife whether he be alive or dead.

Woodcut of a rough band – a form of public punishment often for marital transgressions. From *Chambers' Book of Days*, 1863.

After several years he would be presumed dead and the woman could remarry; this would of course cause a problem if he returned – which could be resolved with a wife sale.

The right to sell your spouse (husband sales were not unknown) was generally accepted and there was shock in 1837 when the East Riding Sessions in Yorkshire sentenced a man to a month in prison with hard labour for selling, or attempting to sell, his wife.

An account from Burford, Oxfordshire, suggests that the outcome of a sale was not always happy. Here a man paid £25 for another man's wife; his neighbours disapproved of the transaction (and probably other factors in the background to this transaction) so they made 'rough music' for the new couple to show their disapproval; consequently he paid her legal husband £15 to take her back.

By the middle of the nineteenth century this practice was dying out, but survived in a few rural areas. Even so the probable last recorded case was in 1928 when a man in Monmouthshire, Wales, told the magistrates at Blackwood that he had sold his wife for one pound.

Rough music

In often small communities there were certain codes of behaviour and conduct by which people were expected to abide. Although a certain amount of leeway was allowed and blind eyes turned to some transgressions, those who persistently transgressed against those codes or else overstepped the mark were likely to be punished by the community. For example, a certain amount of domestic violence could be tolerated – it is often said that a man could beat his wife as long as he used a stick no thicker than his thumb. However, if he did so persistently he could experience public humiliation through a performance by the 'rough band' outside his house. He might also find himself being burnt in effigy and perhaps rhymes concerning his crimes recited.

Another form of display of community disapproval was to beat a bundle of straw outside his house or even just scattering chaff on the doorstep of his house.

The rough band has already been mentioned in regard to the East Anglian custom of serenading the newly weds after their marriage as a form of celebration and acknowledgement of the marriage. However, as mentioned, it was normally carried out as a punishment, usually for some marital transgression.

Anniversaries

Obviously those getting married will expect the marriage to last 'till death do us part' and celebrate many wedding anniversaries. There is little in folklore or tradition outside of the wedding etiquette books which suggests any form of special celebration or marker for the length of the marriage; even the Victorian writer John Cordy Jeaffreson in his thorough account of marriage (*Brides and Bridals*, 1872) makes no mention of the observation of anniversaries. The wedding books usually list the anniversaries as:

1st – paper (or cotton)	14th – ivory
2nd – cotton (or paper)	15th – crystal
3rd – leather	20th – china
4th – silk	25th – silver
5th – wood	30th – pearl
6th – iron	35th – coral
7th – bronze	40th – ruby
8th – electric (or bronze)	45th – sapphire
9th – ceramic	50th – gold
10th – tin	55th – jade (or emerald)
11th – steel	60th – diamond
12th – linen	75th – diamond (again)
13th – lace	

This list probably owes its compilation more to commercial pressures than any folk tradition, in much the same way that the diamond engagement ring was promoted by the De Beers diamond corporation.

FURTHER READING

Information about the customs and superstitions related to marriage is scattered in many folklore and social history books and journals. The publications listed below are some of the key references used in the compilation of this book and can provide a more detailed study and account of the development of marriage traditions in Great Britain.

Ballard, Linda May. *Forgetting Frolic: Marriage Traditions in Ireland.* The Institute of Irish Studies, University of Belfast and The Folklore Society, 1998.

Charsley, Simon R. *Rite of Marrying: The Wedding Industry in Scotland.* Manchester University Press, 1991.

Charsley, Simon R. *Wedding Cakes and Cultural History.* Routledge, 1992.

Cunnington, Phillis, and Lucas, Catherine. *Costume for Births, Marriages and Death.* A & C Black, 1972.

Gillis, John R. *For Better, For Worse: British Marriages, 1600 to the Present.* Oxford University Press, 1985.

Jeaffreson, John Cordy. *Brides and Bridals.* London, 1872.

Lansdell, Avril. *Wedding Fashions 1860–1980.* Shire Publications, 1983.

MacFarlane, Alan. *Marriage and Love in England: 1300–1840.* Blackwell, Oxford, 1986.

Monger, George P. *Marriage Customs of the World: From Henna to Honeymoons.* ABC-Clio, 2004.

Monsarrat, Ann. *And the Bride Wore ... :The Story of the White Wedding.* Gentry Books, London, 1973.

INDEX